Dying to Live

About Highland Books

Our website is <u>www.highlandbks.com</u> whence you can download our catalogue. We also from time to time post errata. If you wish to inform us of typographical errors, you are welcome to e-mail us at:

errata@highlandbks.com.

Dying to Live

My Fight for a Future and a Family

Fran Burke

with Helen Wilkinson

Highland

Godalming, Surrey

First published in 2002 by Highland Books,
Two High Pines, Knoll Road,
Godalming, Surrey GU7 2EP.

ISBN: 1-897913-63-X

Printed in the UK by Biddles Limited, Guildford

DEDICATION
For my boys, whom I risked everything
to give life to, I offer you my story,
so you will know and understand.

Acknowledgements

Adrian. What you did for me was beyond the role of husband and best friend. Without you I know that things would have turned out so different. You're simply the best and I love you.

Anne. No words of thanks will ever be enough for you.

Professor Goldman and all at the Hammersmith. For your support, care and patience.

Dr. Rose. For putting up with me and my tantrums!

Dr. White. For always acting immediately when I was in need.

Mum and Dad. For always being there. No parents could have done any more.

Joyce and Eddie. For your continual support and total belief in me winning through.

Katherine. For your support and friendship.

Helen. My truest friend from childhood to present day. You did it for me and I can't thank you enough.

Tony and all at Anthony Nolan. What a charity!

Anne, Simon and Harvey – for your belief in this book, invaluable help and advice.

Barbara Porter. For never missing a week without writing to me throughout transplant and way beyond.

Dee. Thank heaven for mates like you!

Everyone who has supported me through these tough years - Lorraine, Eric, Nicky, Penny, colleagues at IBM, family members, the villagers of Sherbourne and Rowington; all the photographers who allowed their pictures to be reproduced in the book and the many more who are too numerous to mention.

Thank You

Contents

Foreword by the Duchess of Kent

Iurge everyone to read this book. It tells the story of a remarkable woman who was diagnosed with leukaemia at the age of 29. Fran was just married, and with her life ahead of her she was not to be deterred from her dream of having children. Amazing the medical profession and against all advice, she postponed treatment until her two sons were born.

Then, and only then, did she bravely submit herself to a long drawn-out and debilitating experience of treatment.

Fran confronted fear with courage, and insecurity with trust, a trust in her family and medical team whose support began then and continues to this day.

Above all, it is her humility that shines through in this book. She writes not for praise or sympathy, but to reassure and enlighten others who find themselves in a similar situation, and who seek guidance at a critical time in their lives.

I am proud to call Fran my friend, I am a better person for knowing her. And I do not forget Adrian her husband, and those two boys Matthew and Sebastian for whom this book is written.

Chapter One

A Bolt from the Blue

CR ED CR ED

I was as empty as it's possible to feel.

A nurse adjusted the *Hickman line* in my chest, her grey uniform bathed in the artificial neon glow of my isolation room. No light could penetrate through the blinds of the single locked window, and I couldn't tell whether it was day or night, winter or spring.

I was so tired. It didn't matter how much the drugs made me sleep – I was too weak to think, speak, or move, and the pain nagged away at my body and my determination. From the hospital bed I heard the constant clatter of metal trolleys and sterilised implements on trays. Occasionally I could just make out faint taxi horns and police sirens, so London life must be going on outside, although I was no part of it. For me, life had stood still at eleven am on 5th May 1995, when they exposed me to total body irradiation.

Then I heard the noise I feared more than any other, the call of a nurse telling patients to stay in their rooms. It meant another patient had died. I heard doors banging shut, and Adrian pulled our blind down. For the third time in a week, they wheeled a trolley down the corridor – ten patients on the ward, three deaths. I had peeped at the last trolley, when I was still able to walk, and seen the white sheet covering someone just like me.

My ears picked up another sound, somewhere in the Hammersmith Hospital I could hear a CD playing. The tumbling of notes down the scale of a piano took me back to a happier, faraway time.

I was thirteen years old, and playing the grand piano at home in Warwickshire. The surroundings couldn't have been more different from the drab tiled walls of this isolation room. In the warm remembered glow, I saw myself against the backdrop of curtained winter windows, with a fire burning in the grate. I was note perfect, playing the theme tune to *Love Story*, that I knew by heart.

Immediately after watching the film's first showing on British television, it had become an obsession. I bought the sheet music and played and played, weeping as I practised, until I knew it from memory. The poignancy of the story stayed with me for days, I loved the romance, and the joy of the young couple who were so much in love. Their idyllic relationship was what I longed for, and just like Ali McGraw, I yearned for a knight in shining armour who would whisk me off my feet and do anything for me.

But her life had gone wrong. Soon after marriage, Ali McGraw was diagnosed with leukaemia, and as she lay dying, her young husband watched helplessly at the bedside. So, twenty years before my own diagnosis, I knew the plot – you get leukaemia, you die. Why should it be any different for me?

It was uncanny how real life had mirrored the story of my favourite film. My knight in shining armour had come true too, and he had been forced to go to hell and back for me.

I let my eyes trace the details of my hospital prison, seeing the get well cards, three or four deep on my pin-board, the drug trolley and the Duchess of Kent's own teddy bear looking back at me with sightless eyes.

'How did it all come to this?' I wept.

* * *

Life had been good to me. I had been out with boys, always preferring settled relationships, and every true friend knew my only ambition was to get married, but to the perfect man. I had a wonderful family, financial security, and an excellent job with IBM, in the days when the company was enormously profitable.

Even before Adrian proposed to me, we had talked about having children. Whenever we visited my brother and his wife, Adrian played with their toddler, and his obvious love of children gave me real pleasure. I knew he was going to make a wonderful father.

Before my diagnosis, Adrian and I had been married for less than two years, and life together had begun perfectly. On our wedding day there wasn't a single cloud on my horizon, the sun shone and made it the warmest day of the year. At the perfect reception, Adrian and I opened the dancing to our special song by the Style Council, 'You're the best thing that ever happened to me.'

The words are still true today, Adrian is the best thing in my life, and nothing we go through will ever change that.

After an idyllic honeymoon in Mauritius we planned our future, we would spend a couple of years together, then have two children. My life was very sweet.

By the early spring of 1991, both our careers were demanding, and we were living in a rented house in Stratford-on-Avon while our new home was finished by the builders.

I was having problems with wisdom teeth, and my dentist referred me to Warwick hospital as a day case to have the teeth removed. I was really anxious to have the operation quickly so we could start trying for a baby.

The dental operation went smoothly, but it quickly became obvious something was wrong. My gums wouldn't heal, and after coming home from hospital I was quite ill. My face swelled like a hamster, and the profuse bleeding continued all evening. Adrian was so worried that he rang Casualty, who advised us to cool my gums with frozen peas, but we couldn't stop the bleeding, and in the middle of the night, Adrian drove me to hospital. In the small hours of the morning, they called out the dental surgeon who had operated on me.

He diagnosed an infection, re-stitched my gums and said, 'It's odd, although infection can occur after surgery, I've never had this happen in my entire career. But the antibiotics should sort things out.'

Adrian and I were surprised, but asked no further questions. Nobody gave us cause for alarm, and no blood tests were taken.

Soon afterwards my gums healed, and almost immediately I conceived a child. In April 1991 I had a positive pregnancy test, and Adrian and I were over the moon.

It's extremely difficult for me to write about what happened next, but I want to share it for the sake of anyone else like me who may be diagnosed with leukaemia. I hope and pray that my own terrible experience will prevent people from suffering, as I did, through ignorance of the facts.

On May 24th I went to the GP clinic for my first check-up and blood test of pregnancy, feeling very happy and excited now the wonderful news was beginning to sink in. After the check-up I went straight on to my office at IBM, and at lunch-time Adrian drove the few miles to our new house to have a word with the builders. He was surprised when the foreman told him a doctor had been to the house that morning saying he urgently needed to get hold of Mrs Burke. The doctor had left a message for me to phone immediately.

As Adrian was telling me, I started to shake and feel a wave of nausea. 'What do you think it is? What can it be?' I asked him over and over.

'Don't panic – just ring the doctor,' he said.

So I picked up my office phone and rang the surgery. I was put straight through to my GP who said, 'We've found an unusual blood count, it's nothing to worry about, but I'd like you to go to Warwick hospital tomorrow morning for more blood tests.'

I made the call at four o'clock in the afternoon, and immediately afterwards I rushed to Adrian at his desk and told him I had to go home early. I was in pieces, and everybody wondered what was the matter, as I flung papers into my briefcase and left the office without any explanation.

Adrian followed me to our rented house and tried to calm me down, 'We need to ring the GP again and ask him more questions. I'll do the talking,' he said.

We sat on the settee side by side, and Adrian dialled the surgery. The receptionist put us through to our GP immediately.

'Can you tell us what's in the blood test?' Adrian asked the doctor.

I sat and shivered, despite the warmth of the spring weather. I kept thinking over and over, 'I'm more than ten weeks pregnant, I'm pregnant and I want this baby.'

I couldn't hear what the doctor was saying, but Adrian repeated, 'Right, so there's a high white cell count.'

Straight away, I said out loud, 'I've got leukaemia.'

I knew because of *Love Story*. Although I was only thirteen when I first watched the film, I could remember this part so clearly. Ali McGraw was struggling to conceive a child and went for blood tests to find out what was wrong. The doctor told her she had a high white blood cell count. I could even remember the phrase the doctor had used, telling her the white cells were like an army and they were taking her over.

Adrian was still talking to the doctor and I said again out loud, 'Well that's it, I've got leukaemia.'

Adrian repeated into the receiver, 'Fran's saying it's leukaemia.'

The GP was very professional and reassured him that it was impossible to guess anything at this stage, but we should go to the hospital at eight o'clock next morning and see the consultant who would be able to tell us much more.

I didn't ring anyone. That night was a living hell. I felt absolutely ill, and we sat close together in silence, holding hands and staring into space.

Early next morning we got up and took the dogs for a walk along the riverbank in Stratford – a favourite place of ours – and a thousand questions were going round in my head, 'What am I about to find out, what are they going to tell me? Could they have got the result wrong?'

But I didn't say a word, we walked silently, hand in hand. I had never been so frightened in my life, whatever was wrong with me I knew it must mean disaster, because I was pregnant.

That morning I had a meeting scheduled at the office, and I wasn't even strong enough to ring and make my apologies, I couldn't pick up the phone, so on top of my other fears, I kept worrying about letting IBM down too.

At the hospital I was shocked when we were immediately shown into a side room.

Dr Rose, the consultant haematologist, came to us and said, 'So Mrs Burke, you have a very high white blood cell count – it's over 400 – whereas a normal count is between 5 and 10. We need to find out what's causing this by taking a bone marrow test from your hip. It's painful, a bit like having a tiny corkscrew into your bone, but we do it under local anaesthetic, and it's not too bad.'

He lied, because it was very bad. That first time was the worst, especially as I'm absolutely and completely terrified of hospitals. I've had a blind, irrational fear of them since I went into casualty with a chipped elbow when I was eight years old. Then all they did was X-ray my arm, but I screamed and hollered for every second I was there. The panic induced by the smell, sterility and fear of what they might do to me, is as real today as it was all those years ago.

I wouldn't let Adrian out of my sight. He held my hand while the bone marrow sample was taken, then we had to sit and wait for the sample to be analysed. My hip and my heart were both aching because I knew deep down that I had leukaemia.

It seemed to take hours until Dr Rose came back to us. 'I'm afraid you've got leukaemia,' he said, without any warning or preamble. I guess there's no nice way to say it.

I was still and cold as stone. Straight away I asked him, 'Am I going to die?'

The doctor started to talk in circles, with a meandering, general sort of answer. He mentioned transplants and donors and I stopped listening. I thought to myself, 'He isn't saying no, so that must mean I could die.'

'Am I going to die?'

'No. I mean, there's a possibility you could die, but we'll look for a donor, there's a donor register, then we can consider a bone marrow transplant …'

I butted in, 'What about my baby?'

'We don't need to worry about that at the moment. We'll sort out some treatment for you, but there's no hurry.'

He had told me the high white cell count was a problem for me, but had made no mention of it being a concern for our unborn child. He said 'You have a condition called Chronic Myeloid Leukaemia which is pretty rare and tends to affect adults more than children.'

I wasn't listening, and Adrian was leaning forward and staring into space.

Dr Rose could see there was no point going on. 'There's plenty of time to go into details later, I'll leave you alone to let you get used to what I've said,' and he left us.

A nurse brought me a cup of tea and I can remember crying out loud, hysterically, while Adrian sat in silence and hugged me tight. Then he cried too, but I was absolutely inconsolable.

Suddenly I thought 'That's why they put me in this room – because they knew.' 'Why me?' I screamed, 'Why us?'

'That's wasted energy – you can't afford to ask why,' Adrian said through his tears. 'You've got to channel all your energy into conquering this. I know you'll get through, we're not going to let anything happen to you, so we'll look forward and fight and never, ever give up.'

I looked up at his hot, red face and saw a fire of love and determination in his eyes. He was amazing, his support for me began at the moment the diagnosis was given.

After a while he encouraged me to go into the office, knowing that we would cope better by doing something.

'We'll get through this whatever happens – we'll get on top of it Fran.'

Chapter Two

Facing the Music

ଔ ଯ ଔ ଯ

Wе drove straight to IBM in a state of complete shock. Adrian took control of the situation and I felt weak, empty, and numb. He called my account team together for an emergency meeting. We sat in the little conference room that I had used dozens of times for sales meetings and team briefings, and my colleagues were laughing and joking just like any other day.

'And what time do you call this to roll into the office!' one quipped.

'This had better be good, because I was about to have a coffee!'

'Fran and Adrian calling a team meeting; it must be something major!'

My boss was out of the office, but we sat down with my team, five men and me, and I couldn't make a single word come out of my mouth.

So Adrian did all the talking, 'We've come straight from the hospital where Fran has just been told she's got leukaemia. We don't understand what it means, and we don't know the implications for her job or time commitments, but she won't be in work today. She needs to get to grips with the news. We'll keep you informed as soon as we know anything.'

No-one said a word. For the first time in any IBM meeting of my career, there was absolute silence. My team didn't ask a single question, I guess they were gob-smacked. All the bravado of youth and confidence had deserted them.

Adrian said, 'We'll tell my manager and then we'll be leaving – please cancel all Fran's meetings for the day.'

'Fine, fine, take as much time as you need,' they said. It felt very awkward.

Adrian's manager couldn't have been kinder when we told him, and said 'I'm so sorry and shocked – take as much time off work as you like. Don't worry about IBM at all.'

Within the company, there was a lot of support for us as a couple. Many of our colleagues had become friends, and we were well-known as the young newly-weds who worked in the same IBM branch. The staff teased us good-naturedly for our devotion to each other, and our managers were always very good to us. In the lead up to the wedding, everyone had been rooting for us. That support came to mean so much to us as my illness progressed.

Adrian and I left by the familiar walkway out of the white and glass building and I said, 'Drive me to Mum's. I want to tell her now, I don't want to wait until Dad comes home from work, I need to tell her straight away.'

Mum was in the study at the family home where I had grown up. The piano where I learned to play *Love Story* was standing silent as it had done since my wedding.

I told her the news very simply. She was typical Mum, her world must have started to rock, but she said 'Right, we've got to work out what must be done. We'll get you the best treatment, and you and the baby will be fine.'

I knew she was holding herself together for me and I loved her more than ever for that.

We went on to my father's office unannounced, which I'd never done in my life. He came out of his office smiling and said, 'Come on in then, what's so serious that you need to see me here?'

Just as my colleagues at IBM had done, Dad was making a joke of it.

We sat opposite Dad on the other side of his desk and I said, 'I've been diagnosed with leukaemia. The baby is OK, and there's no indication that we'll have a problem. We've told Mum and I reckon she'd like you to go home.'

In contrast to Mum's reaction, Dad was quiet, he seemed to be mulling it over instead of speaking, letting the terrible facts sink in.

Adrian and I didn't know what to do next, and ended up at our new house which the builders had almost finished, knowing there would be plenty of jobs to occupy our minds. When we arrived, Adrian went to talk to the builders.

I stood alone in the drive and looked at the tall horse-chestnut trees, decked in full May blossom, and I wept helplessly. The beauty of the spring trees hit me like a thunder-bolt, and I thought, 'It's so beautiful – nature is so impossibly beautiful and I don't appreciate it, I've been through life without appreciating things like this. Now I may never see another spring.' No sight would ever be more beautiful to me, or so precious.

There was a paddock adjoining the new garden and I walked around it, lost in thought and tears, then wandered into the house. The ceiling of the lounge was open to the new rafters, and I sat on a breeze block in the middle of the floor, while Adrian worked overhead, threading electric cables that would supply power to the hi-fi. I thought about my life, and the tiny baby inside me, and nothing made sense. My ignorance about this illness was absolute, I knew nothing about leukaemia or its treatment. That day, I just thought about life and its meaning, and about death too.

The only comfort I had in those first days was Adrian. After the moment of diagnosis in the hospital room, he never broke down. He got me through. I owe my life to a lot of people and several reasons, but without Adrian I couldn't have begun. Countless times I have thought that if I had never met or married Adrian, my life may have turned out very differently. No man could have been better for me, with me, to me – my love and gratitude to him cannot be expressed.

That night, I phoned my brother Nick and said 'I've got some good and bad news.'

'Let's have the good news.'

'I'm pregnant.'

'That's wonderful – so what's the bad news?'

'I've got leukaemia – I don't know what it means, but it's not good news.'

Then I rang my best friend. We didn't mention the pregnancy to anyone outside the family, this book is the first time I have spoken about that part of my story.

I woke very early the next morning to the sound of birds singing the dawn chorus. With a wave of sickening realisation, I remembered I wasn't dreaming; yesterday I was diagnosed with leukaemia.

Later I had a phone call from my GP, Dr White, who said, 'I'll be here for you and support every decision you make, but I'll be honest and admit I don't know anything about your illness. I've never had a patient with leukaemia in my surgery, and you need a specialist for the times when I can't answer your questions.'

I really appreciated him saying that, over the past ten years I've learned the medical profession gain your trust by being honest even when the news is bad, saying they don't know is often the best answer.

My GP recommended a haematologist to take on my case and we assumed he must be one of the top people as he worked in Birmingham, and we were grateful for our GP's thoughtfulness. In those early days we made no attempt to do our own research, but were pulled along by events, and thankful for any offers of help.

At our first consultation with the haematologist, his knowledge of leukaemia was obvious, and he began to give us details about the illness. I was in a strange state of confusion, not wanting to hear a single word because that made it more real, but at the same time desperate to understand what we were facing.

The haematologist said, 'You have Chronic Myeloid Leukaemia, Fran, known as CML. It is impossible to know the cause, and you may have had it for months or even years without detection. Leukaemia is cancer of the blood which starts in the bone marrow, the factory where blood cells are made.'

Adrian did all the talking for both of us, 'What's the prognosis for someone with CML?'

'It's very difficult to be precise, because we never know when the patient contracted it, only when it was diagnosed, but experience shows that the chronic phase of the disease usually lasts for five or six years.'

'What happens after that?'

'It's not always five years – I must emphasise that – because in some cases the chronic phase lasts only months, in others much longer than five years. But at some time the condition converts from chronic to acute. I'll try and explain the disease for you.'

The haematologist lined up two pots and a stapler on his desk. 'Human blood consists of a number of different types of cell and we need all of them to function properly. We have red blood cells containing haemoglobin and they carry oxygen around the body.' He moved a red pot. 'Then we have platelets which allow our blood to clot when we have an injury. And we have white blood cells which help the body to overcome infection.' He moved the stapler and a white pot of paper clips around on his shiny desk. 'These different blood cells are contained in normal blood in perfect equilibrium and are constantly produced and replaced.

'Like every cell in our bodies, our blood cells contain chromosomes inherited from our parents. In Fran's case, for some unknown reason she has developed a defect in one chromosome which has produced a faulty gene called the BCRABL gene.'

It was beginning to go over my head, but I looked at Adrian and he was absolutely gripped, taking in every word.

'The defective BCRABL gene causes the number of white blood cells to increase. It produces a protein that prevents white cells reaching maturity, and too many white cells are produced – they can't function properly and can't fight infection.' He tipped out the paper clips all over his desk and spread them about. 'Pretty quickly everything starts to go wrong, and the balance of the blood is upset. There isn't enough room for the red cells so the patient can become anaemic, feel tired, have trouble breathing from lack of oxygen, or bruise easily. And the lack of room for platelets means you can't stop bleeding. That's why your gums couldn't heal after dental surgery Fran.'

As he spoke I stared at the pots and clips on his desk and imagined my own blood. I had never, ever thought about it before, but now I could almost sense my veins and arteries. In every part of me I pictured bad blood flowing, and dreaded the side effects he described. I felt as though I had been taken over by an invisible enemy and I wanted to destroy it.

Adrian asked 'You mentioned going acute, what happens then?'

'After a period of time, usually from three to six years, the leukaemia transforms from chronic to acute and the immature white blood cells turn into blast cells and spread rapidly through the body. Death can be very quick and sudden at that stage, and a bone marrow transplant performed after acute transformation has a poor chance of success. That's why we always try to arrange a transplant in the chronic phase, as soon as possible after diagnosis.'

Death. He had brought up the subject. I sat very still and cold.

'But maybe Fran's won't go acute?' asked Adrian desperately.

'I'm afraid that's impossible. All cases of CML turn acute, every single one. It's only a matter of time, but it's a certainty.'

'I see,' said Adrian, 'then we have to find a donor for a transplant.'

The haematologist suggested I should take a drug called *Hydoroxyurea* to slow down the rate of formation of my white cells. It couldn't cure leukaemia, no drug could do that, but could limit the harmful effect of the immature white cells, and restore the natural blood balance. He glossed over any harmful effect it would have on my baby and showed no concern for the pregnancy at all. Later on I was to discover that *Hydoroxyurea* slows down cell division and stops the growth of a baby in early pregnancy.

The haematologist was working from an assumption the baby couldn't live, and that I couldn't survive a pregnancy without treatment.

I agreed to take the drug because he told me I had no choice. It was presented to me as a life or death decision. It took me three years to learn that sometimes the medics get it wrong.

The haematologist said 'Your white cell count is rising and at 400, it's very, very high already. The cell count can only go up, and as you're in such early stages of pregnancy, your chances of survival to a full term of nine months are worse than slim.'

I looked at him in silence. I had no strength to do more than blink and breathe.

'But we can't do a termination of the pregnancy at the moment either, it would be too dangerous because your high white cell count and lack of platelets increases the danger of a haemorrhage.'

He had said it, the word 'termination' hung in the air between us and polluted my feeling for the man.

He went on, 'So I want you to take the *Hydoroxyurea* for a few weeks while the white cell count comes down, then you must terminate the pregnancy.'

This was the very worst news in the world for me. Not only was I being told I was dying, but that my baby couldn't survive. We left the surgery and I began a period of emotional shut-down which lasted for weeks.

Chapter Three

My Perfect Man

Three days after my diagnosis was our second wedding anniversary. Before we heard the news I had booked a couple of nights Bed and Breakfast together in North Devon. When we married we had agreed to take turns booking an anniversary surprise for each other, and this year it was my surprise. But now I couldn't bring myself to go anywhere, how could I celebrate our wedding anniversary when everything was falling apart?

My parents were adamant that a change of scene would help us, and Adrian and I drove to Devon with the *Hydoroxyurea* tablets packed in my weekend bag.

Once we arrived in the pretty village, we didn't know what to do with ourselves.

That evening at dinner, as soon as my main course was put in front of me, I said 'I'm going to be ill. I've got to go out.'

The restaurant was cosily small so I felt utterly conspicuous and embarrassed. I walked around in the fresh air outside the building, taking deep breaths and trying to pull myself together.

When I came back inside, I begged Adrian to eat my meal for me, the plateful of food was giving me feelings of complete panic. I was longing to go back to the hotel bedroom and be left alone.

We couldn't face touring or seeing the sights, so next day we drove to Exmoor, parked the car and read the papers. I sat with the *Daily Mail* open on my knee and couldn't read a single word. We sat in the car for two hours altogether, Adrian reading, and me staring blankly at the newsprint. My heart was breaking.

I thought about the diagnosis, and wondered what may have happened in the past to cause this, fearing what lay ahead, and aching inside.

The bleak, empty scenery mirrored my mind, and I looked at it without seeing any meaning in life. I tried to remember the joy of my past, and throughout those two hours on Exmoor, I retraced my life with Adrian.

We had met in Manchester during a one-day course with IBM, part of my training for a career as a Systems Engineer (or SE – acronyms are part of life in IBM). Adrian was on the front row of the classroom and I was at the back, giving me a perfect opportunity to watch him unawares. He was exactly my type, tall and slim with dark hair, an honest face and cheeky eyes. During morning coffee break we met at the drinks machine.

'Hi!' was all I could manage. That was as much as passed our lips.

All through the afternoon session, while the tutor explained the finer points of System 390, I kept glancing at this dark-haired, good-looking IBM-er in the front row. I felt certain he must have a lovely girlfriend, but I knew he was just the sort of guy I wanted to meet and marry. Even though I knew nothing about him at all, those were the very thoughts going through my head.

We didn't speak again, and he returned to his office in Manchester.

In those days, my only brother Nick also worked for IBM Manchester. After the training course, I called in to meet Nick, and to my amazement, the good-looking stranger was sitting at my brother's double desk.

'Hi, I was looking for Nick.'

'He's in a meeting. Do you want to wait, or can I help?'

'Not really, he's my brother and we're meeting for supper.' I paused and gathered my thoughts, 'What are you doing here?'

'I'm your brother's new SE – we're working on the Barclays account together. I've just finished SE school in Portsmouth and this is my first assignment.'

'Why did you come up to Manchester?'

'Financially it was a good offer, and it'll be great having more money so I can spend it on my girlfriend.'

My heart sank, and I couldn't think of anything else to say. Nick appeared from his meeting and I went to supper, thinking sadly of what might have been.

When we'd eaten, Nick said, 'I'm surprised you don't fancy my new SE, Adrian Burke, I'd have thought he was just your type.'

The summer came and went, and one day in September I had a Noss note (an IBM precursor of email) from Adrian saying, 'Hi! Remember me? I'm coming to Warwick on business – do you fancy dinner tonight?'

I sent back 'Free nosh – sounds great!' and we met for a bar meal.

By the end of the evening I felt brave enough to ask him about his girlfriend.

'What girlfriend?'

'The one you said you were looking forward to spending more money on.'

'I wasn't referring to a specific girl. I was meaning girls in general, it's nice to have money to spend on girlfriends plural.'

We went back to my flat and talked until four in the morning. I told him about my past relationships and he talked about his own. I felt such relief that he was single, and my hopes soared, though we hadn't even kissed.

After that he sent me cards in the post, saying 'Hiya sexy!' and telling me he'd wanted to approach me at the training course but had assumed I must be engaged or unobtainable. He sent me cassettes of his favourite music and we exchanged regular emails.

But we weren't going out together, nothing had happened. So I invited him to join me for a weekend in London for the IBM exhibition. My timing was lousy, because he had just bought a house and was due to collect the keys and move in that weekend. But Adrian said he would come anyway, and I realised he must be keen to see me.

We agreed to meet at the hotel where I was staying with my team of colleagues. When Adrian arrived, reception put out several tannoys but I didn't hear them above the noise of the bar where I was sitting with the IBM group.

While he was waiting for me to respond, by coincidence Adrian bumped into an ex-girlfriend in reception who was on her way to a Halloween party and invited him to join her. Before giving up on me and going to the party, Adrian decided to tannoy one last time.

In the bar I thought I heard my name, and went to reception.

It's funny how your life can turn on a single moment. That was the night we started going out together.

From the very first day I was head over heels in love. Throughout the months we dated, I had my head in the clouds, and was swept off my feet by the romance.

And I needed reassurance – I'd lacked confidence from my earliest days, at school and at work. Despite my happy childhood, I was insecure and uncertain of myself. A cool, detached romance would have been torture for me – I craved reassurance and love. Adrian showered me with love and affection and made me feel totally special.

I even had a bet with my best friend who said we'd be engaged within six months. For a girl like me who never ever bets, this was a serious business.

We had a coded message 'Ra Ra Ra!' which meant 'I love you.' On Valentine's Day he brought me red roses and the daily paper. I scanned the Valentine messages and saw 'To Fran – Ra Ra Ra!'

I put the paper down and smiled up at him.

For the first time, he dropped the code, 'I love you,' he said.

Seven months after the Halloween weekend, on 14th May 1988, Adrian proposed. We had bought two West Highland puppies together and we spent every weekend with the dogs in my flat in Leamington, or Adrian's house in Manchester.

That Saturday Adrian said, 'Let's go to the Burton Dassett Hills and walk the dogs.'

When we had walked for a while he said, 'Sit down, close your eyes and hold out your hands.'

'This had better be a cream egg because I'm absolutely starving.'

I opened my eyes and saw a small box. Until that moment I hadn't suspected a thing, and I was truly gob-smacked. Adrian was silent. I opened the box and saw a perfect diamond solitaire, and then he asked me to marry him.

'Absolutely, yes, yes, yes!' I said.

I was over the moon, on cloud nine, you could trot out all the clichés in the world for perfect happiness, and they would all apply to that moment.

We both applied for internal transfers and I volunteered to move to Manchester, but when Adrian was offered a good job at IBM Warwick, we decided it was better for him to move south and make my new home ours.

All four parents were delighted, particularly my Mum and Dad who were mostly relieved for the puppies.

Mum said, 'Thank goodness my grand-pups aren't going to have a broken home! We love Adrian already, and we knew from the start that you were made for each other.'

It never occurred to me that we may not be able to have children, and as soon as we married, I was desperately keen to start trying for a family. I was already twenty-six, and had this crazy notion that time was running out, some of my closest friends were already mothers or pregnant at the very least.

We had talked endlessly about having a family, even before the wedding. Adrian was an only child and hoped for two boys who would be able to share the companionship he sometimes missed.

I remember vividly one conversation at a pub when we were engaged. We were talking about the future and Adrian said, 'Obviously when we have a family you'll want to be a housewife and give up work.'

'What do you mean "obviously"? I've got a career and I've got no intention of giving up and sitting at home being a housewife!'

Adrian was genuinely surprised by my reaction, 'I'm amazed Fran, I always thought you would want to be the one to bring up the children, but whatever you want is fine.'

How little we knew about the shocks ahead that would turn our world and our plans upside down.

Two years after the wedding Adrian and I had agreed it was time to start trying for a child. Right here was the place our decision had led us, sitting in the car, with Exmoor drizzle streaming down the windscreen, and pain seeping into my heart.

Now even the memories of our past couldn't touch or console me. What was the point of it all? I had met the perfect man, had a wonderful family and a good job, but nothing in my world could save me. I had everything to live for, but no bridge into the future. Other people were still driving their cars and eating picnics as though the world was normal, and today was just like any other day.

As dinner time approached, I got more and more screwed up and told Adrian I couldn't face a single mouthful of food. We said nothing to the staff, and I sat at the dinner table wishing I was anywhere but there.

We didn't talk much, in those early days we didn't know enough about the condition to have detailed discussions, but

I remember asking Adrian, 'What do you think caused my leukaemia? What did I do wrong?'

'At the end of the day it doesn't matter what caused it Fran, don't spend all your time worrying about how it started. Now we're in the situation there's no point looking back, so we're going to look forwards, whatever happens.'

We were both in shock, and experienced a new level of closeness. Fear of losing each other brought us a sense of preciousness that I'd never felt before.

The very worst part of the weekend was taking the tablets prescribed by the haematologist. I feared taking drugs of any kind, and had never even had a tablet for a headache, but that weekend I had to force myself to take the very first dose, and as soon as I swallowed it, I wanted to vomit it up. Each time I swallowed one of the small white pills, I hated what it was doing to me and my baby. Even though I'd been told I couldn't have the child, I knew it was still alive and growing and I was afraid every tablet may be hurting it.

These bitter, heart-breaking days were darker for me than any time I ever faced later on. I endured pain and agony for myself in the years to come, and that was easy in comparison. Nothing comes close to the grief I carried from harming our first baby, a grief that no time will ever take away.

Adrian had always promised me an eternity ring, and had said it would make an apt present for our tenth wedding anniversary. In the bed and breakfast where we had planned to make our celebrations so special, I jokingly said, 'Look here Ade, I'm not waiting ten years for this ring, so get a move on!' We've actually had many wedding anniversaries since then, but the sense of sadness is always part of the celebrations even now, it's become an anniversary not only of our wedding, but of my diagnosis.

From that time onwards my blood was tested and the white cell count monitored once a week. It remained static for a while, and then started to come down.

The haematologist explained they don't know why in some people the chromosome deforms and CML begins, it may be caused by a seemingly innocent virus in the past that triggered the irreversible mutation. There may be a link with living near radiation, but it has never been proved, and in my case wasn't a possibility.

The BCRABL gene was generating excessive numbers of white blood cells, which kept dividing and multiplying, and nothing but a bone marrow transplant would stop that, by killing the deformed cells and starting afresh with normal healthy bone marrow from the donor.

There are many forms of leukaemia, and several variants between the forms common in both adult or childhood. Children tend to be diagnosed with Acute Myeloid Leukaemia which is often treatable with chemotherapy followed by a transplant if chemotherapy fails. Thankfully there's a high success rate for the treatment of Acute Myeloid Leukaemia. CML is a rare form, quite unusual in young adults, and more commonly diagnosed in late middle age. But it is also one of the most dangerous forms you can have as an adult, and I was counting down inexorably to the day when the condition would turn acute.

Despite the danger, Adrian was always positive and kept talking about the future when I would be well again. One evening in those dark, black days, I just lost my patience with his optimism. He had made another hopeful comment and I decided to pick a fight with him. 'I don't think you've taken it in, because whatever they bash at me you never break down, you just say, "right, now we've got to move on". Well I can't move on.' I was screaming now, 'You've not accepted it, you're burying your head in the sand. I've got bloody leukaemia for God's sake!'

Adrian was very quiet and looked indescribably sad. 'Fran, there are times when I think about the future from every angle, and I ask the obvious questions like "I can't believe this has happened, why us?" Sometimes when I'm mowing the lawn and it's a beautiful day, I imagine what it would be like to lose you, and I long for us to be just like any normal couple, but that isn't going to help either of us. You need me and you need my support, and there's so much for us to look forward to. I'm an optimist by nature, which doesn't mean I don't face reality, but I'm confident you'll make it through, and that always comes to the surface. So don't tell me I haven't faced it, I have, and I'm fighting for both of us.'

I was crying hot tears of love and anger as he spoke.

'I love you Fran, even more now because of this, and we're going to make it,' he said.

The haematologist said he was waiting for my cell count to drop to a level safe enough for me to have surgery, and then he was adamant I must terminate the pregnancy. It was at this stage he chose to tell me about the harmful effects of *Hydoroxyurea* on the baby. He explained that the drug had taken my options away, and the baby had no future. Its growth would now be deformed and I had no choice but to abort it.

I reeled, and although I had believed him when he first told me the baby couldn't survive, I had extreme difficulty coping with the news now. I knew there was a life growing inside me and it felt desperately wrong allowing it to continue developing, which could only make a termination harder. My state of mind declined very fast and nothing could rouse me or make me forget the baby.

It's funny but I actually came to terms with the leukaemia diagnosis relatively quickly. What I couldn't handle was the loss of my unborn child. Perhaps when the haematologist considered my case, he saw only my leukaemia, but when I looked at the situation, I saw only the child. We were both coming at the problem from a different perspective, and that disparity led to a greater tragedy in the end.

My parents were very worried as they watched me go downhill. It had been an ambition of a lifetime for me to go to Wimbledon, and that summer my father had been given centre court tickets by a client. Out of love and concern for me, Dad asked the client whether I could go to Wimbledon with Mum in his place, knowing it would give me something to look forward to. The business colleague agreed and I actually started to feel a little bit of interest.

After a few short weeks, the haematologist declared me safe for surgery and said he would arrange the hospital bed for a termination. I asked him to avoid the day at Wimbledon, and he promised he would, but when he rang to confirm the termination, it was booked for my day at Centre Court. I was gutted, feeling he simply didn't care what I was going through, but he said it was the only date he could offer. My parents had worked hard to give me the treat and the idea had been thrown back in their face.

This was bad enough, but to make matters worse, in the week before the termination, a senior colleague from IBM rang and asked me to be his witness at his civil wedding on the following Thursday. My operation was booked for the Tuesday.

I was completely surprised to be invited, and the phone call was very awkward. I explained that I was having a very minor operation involving a general anaesthetic two days before the wedding, but that I would get there for him. Then he told me the wedding was extremely small so Adrian wasn't included in the invitation, as there wouldn't be room.

He pushed me for a definite answer on the phone and I was so traumatised that I gave in and agreed to go alone.

I put down the phone and turned to Adrian, 'I can't go without you, I can't,' and broke down, completely upset and lost. My baby was dying, I may not survive and I felt absolutely alone.

Adrian said, 'Ring back and ask him if I can come.'

So I picked up the phone again and dialled.

The groom was very awkward, 'Fran, I must emphasise that the wedding is tiny, it isn't fair on anyone else if I agree to an extra guest.'

'But, Adrian will have to drive me to the wedding because of my anaesthetic, so can't you just make one exception for him, please?'

It wasn't easy to persuade him. He knew about my diagnosis, but I guess he had no idea what I was going through. In the end he agreed Adrian could come. It was a bizarre situation at an impossible time.

The next Tuesday, when I was fourteen weeks pregnant, Adrian drove me to hospital for the termination. It was another bleak and terrifying place, and the staff made me feel like one more in a long line of careless girls who wanted a convenience abortion. And even if that were my situation, I knew they had no right to treat me that way. I felt angry and bitterly upset.

A nurse tossed a green gown to me and asked, 'Have you had a bath or shower this morning?' That was her only concern.

'Yes, as I told you, I had a shower an hour ago at home.'

'Well I'd like you to have another one.'

'No, I don't want one, I don't need one!' My anger spilled out of me towards this fractious, unsympathetic woman. I knew she had never been forced to choose between dying and losing her baby, and for a moment I wanted her and all the staff to know what it felt like. But I didn't say another word.

When I came round from the anaesthetic, I was weepy and felt desperate. The haematologist was in hospital because he had been worried I may haemorrhage, and he'd arranged for me to be in a room on my own. He examined me after the operation and said I was out of danger and could be discharged.

Adrian drove me to our little rented house in Stratford and I went straight to bed and cried and cried without stopping. My parents came over and I couldn't pull myself together even for them. I remember my mother saying to Dad, 'It's the worst thing that can happen to a woman, losing her baby,' but Dad didn't know how to console me.

And two days later was my colleague's wedding. I tried to get a grip of myself and put on a mask of happiness for him. I knew I had to get through the day, but I was still weak and feeling ill from the anaesthetic and frightened of being centre of attention as his witness. The entire day was a living hell, and I couldn't have got through it without Adrian beside me, touching my waist with his hand to reassure me he was there, and knew what I was suffering.

I smiled and pretended, and the minutes ticked through the ceremony and lunch in the tiny garden. The other witness wanted me to go indoors and help her do an apple pie bed and put confetti in the luggage, so I held myself together and faked a joviality I didn't feel. I watched the hand moving on the face of my watch until eventually it was late enough for us to escape without looking rude.

It may seem odd, but that day was almost as bad as the day of the termination. For me, life had lost all charm and meaning, and I had no wish to be part of it. I couldn't imagine that I'd ever be the same again. The sun shone and summer bloomed all around me, but I had shrivelled up inside like a dead thing.

No-one had mentioned that leukaemia would prevent me from having a baby in the future. I had no idea how long I may live, or whether I'd ever have a chance to get pregnant. I had no idea what lay ahead, and for a while after the baby was gone, I went to pieces. I didn't know which way to turn and didn't really care what happened to me.

There was one silver lining to the cloud: a week after my termination, Dad confided in his business colleague about my leukaemia and the kind man offered centre court tickets at Wimbledon for Adrian and I as a get-well gift. It was a happy day in the blackest of times.

FOOTPRINTS
by Margaret Fishback Powers

One night I dreamed a dream.
I was walking along the beach with my Lord.
Across the dark sky flashed scenes from my life.
For each scene, I noticed two sets
of footprints in the sand,
one belonging to me
and one to my Lord.
When the last scene of my life shot before me,
I looked back at the footprints in the sand.
There was only one set of footprints.
I realised that this was at the lowest
and saddest times of my life.
This always bothered me
and I questioned the Lord
about my dilemma.
'Lord, you told me when I decided to follow you,
you would walk and talk with me all the way.
But I'm aware that during the most troublesome
times of my life, there is only one set of footprints.
I just don't understand why, when I needed you most,
you leave me.'
He whispered, 'My precious child,
I love you and will never leave you
never, ever, during your trials and testings.
When you saw only one set of footprints,
it was then that I carried you.'

Chapter Four

Turning the Corner

ন ৯ ন ৯

On top of an overwhelming grief, I had two dominant emotions at this time; guilt and moral confusion. I hated myself for what I had done to our child, and believed I had no right to ever having another baby.

Then I discovered the terrible truth that after a transplant I would be unable to have children. The radiation involved would kill off many organs and tissues, including my ovaries, leaving me sterile.

I couldn't reconcile the two terrible opposites, I had killed a baby – yet I longed for a family with Adrian. The only treatment was a bone marrow transplant, which would make a family impossible. So I had to choose between my life and a child, a vicious brain-teaser that I could never solve.

Adrian was wonderful with me throughout this awful time, I talked incessantly about the termination, and went over and over the same ground in our night-time conversations. Looking back, I was asking for reassurance about what we had been forced to do, and confirmation we could still have a child.

But whatever he said gave me no comfort, and I just couldn't move on. I needed answers from a higher authority, and perhaps with the benefit of hindsight, I wanted to know the mind of God. We went round in circles, until Adrian suggested we go and see our local vicar Brian Ritchie for advice. We attended church regularly, and we both share a simple but deep faith in God.

Adrian phoned him and asked 'Could Fran and I come and have a chat with you?'

'Of course, I'd be delighted,' Brian replied.

We met at the vicarage and he showed us into his study. I tried to tell Brian everything that had happened and poured out my feelings of guilt and shame and fear. It felt as therapeutic as talking to a counsellor, and Brian couldn't have been more understanding. He sat and listened, only nodding and affirming all that I said and cried.

His empathy was obvious; 'Poor you,' he said over and over, 'it must have been such a terrible time for you both.' Like everyone else, he had known only the public side of our story, and although that was bad enough, the truth was worse.

When I had finished pouring out my feelings, Brian didn't push religion at me, but he gave some very deep and reassuring messages. 'I can't give you simple answers Fran, life in the modern world is horribly complicated. There are so many things we can't explain, there's so much suffering and pain, and life sometimes seems very unfair.

'All I can do is re-affirm that God loves you, and he loved your baby too. It is very clear to me how much you want to have a child. Pray about it, and if your heart is telling you to have another baby, then that's not wrong. It sounds as though your yearning for a child will never, ever go away.

'You can't blame yourself for the rest of your life for what happened, and you need to move on, for your own sake, and for Adrian. If a child is the way forward, then so be it. But remember one thing: God loves you and that will never, ever change. However much you loved your baby, God loves you more.'

While Brian was speaking I felt a weight lifting from my weary body. I didn't know what I was expecting him to say, and can't explain why I went to the vicar for an answer.

Maybe I saw him as a figure of authority who would give me a simple 'yes' or 'no' to the most complex of questions. Or maybe it was an example of turning to God at our lowest times, and through Brian, God helped me profoundly.

Although the sense of guilt didn't leave, and never will, I came out of the vicarage thinking, 'No, it isn't wrong to want a child.'

Adrian and I talked everything through immediately, and both felt utterly convinced that a loving God would not withhold the love of a family from us. That meeting was instrumental in my recovery from the termination and I am very thankful to Brian for his part in the process. That was the turning point, from which our resolution was born, to do everything we could to have a baby before a transplant.

I was still taking *Hydoroxyurea*, and although I hated it, the drug had done a good job of bringing my white cell count down, and I continued to see the haematologist regularly. But, despite my fear of anything medical, when I needed treatment or tests, he would never let Adrian stay with me. He always insisted Adrian wait outside. So my fear and dread increased with every appointment.

At the first consultation after the termination he said, 'There's another drug called *Alpha Interferon* which I think you should try. It's expensive and you have to inject it into your stomach every day, but there have been recent trials suggesting it may actually control leukaemia for many years in about five per cent of cases. It has the potential to work on the deformed chromosome and significantly alter the blood ratio, bringing down the white cell count.'

I looked at Adrian for reassurance.

'It sounds worth a try,' he said.

'But I can't inject myself, I can't do that.'

'I'll help you Fran, it's got to be worth trying if there's a chance it may help you.'

So the haematologist showed us how to use it, and while he was demonstrating, Adrian suddenly said 'I've got to sit down,' and went faint.

We took the *Interferon* home and the very first time Adrian injected into my tummy, he felt dizzy again. But he was strong and patient, and every day he encouraged me to watch what he was doing, and eventually, after practising on an orange, I had a go myself. It hurt every single time, and before long my stomach was covered in bruises, but I learned to do it.

Although I had felt well until that point, once I started taking *Interferon*, I began to feel ill. I was tired and had lost all my energy, with spasmodic pains in my limbs and back, often forcing me into hospital. I carried on working throughout, and knew I had changed, but didn't link it to the *Interferon* at that time.

The haematologist began to flesh out the idea of a bone marrow transplant, which was my only hope of a full cure. Put simply, it is a risky procedure involving total body irradiation to kill the defective gene which produces the mutant white blood cells. After irradiation, which takes the patient almost to the point of death, bone marrow is injected into the body from a donor whose genetic blood pattern is very close to the patient's own.

Every person is unique and each of us has a unique genetic code like a fingerprint. For a transplant to work, the donor's bone marrow must be as similar as possible to the patient's, otherwise the incoming immune system will reject the patient's body as foreign.

The very best chance of a successful transplant is with an identical twin, the next best with a sibling, because the genetic fingerprint is inherited from the same parents and therefore has a good chance of matching. Wheels were set in motion to test my brother Nick and my hopes began to soar; I was certain Nick would be a match, enabling a low-risk bone marrow transplant and a full cure. While a transplant from an unrelated donor has on average a 45% chance of success, with a sibling, the probability is as high as 75%.

My brother had a blood test, and when the result was ready, my haematologist called Adrian and I into the familiar consulting room, and I could tell by his body language that it wasn't good news.

He said, 'We've got the result of Nick's blood test, and I'm afraid he isn't a match.'

'How can you be sure from one blood test?' I yelped.

'You and your brother have both inherited different genes from your parents, and we can tell by testing the first four antigens in your brother's blood sample. In all body cells including the blood, each of us has a long string of genes in our genetic code, and for a bone marrow match we test the first four only. The first six antigens are A/A B/B and DR/DR and we were hoping you and Nick had inherited an identical A/A and B/B combination from your parents. There was a twenty-five per cent chance you had inherited an identical gene set, but I'm afraid to say you've been unlucky.'

'Can't you do another test to check?'

'There's absolutely no point. For a transplant we need the first five or six antigens to match, and now we know the first four are different, there's no way we can reach the necessary total of five out of six. Nick isn't a match.'

Tears were rolling down my face, it was only at that moment I realised how much I had been relying on good news. I felt as though I'd been following a signpost to survival but had met only a brick wall ahead. I didn't have any alternatives, there was no fall-back route.

Very early the next morning I went into IBM, trying to catch up with my backlog of work. But despite the pressure of late deadlines, I couldn't concentrate on anything, and sat for a couple of hours staring at the computer screen. People were arriving to begin their working day.

My dear friend John, who had always been very caring, came up to my desk, 'How are you Fran – how's it going?'

I turned my face away from him so he wouldn't see the tears running down my cheeks and trickling off my chin.

'What's the matter?' You can tell me.'

'Nick's not a match!' I sobbed, 'and I don't know what to do.'

'I know how much this means Fran,' he said, wheeling an office chair up to me, 'tell me what happened.'

We sat and talked for a long time, and then John told me to go home and get some rest.

'But what about my job? I'll lose my job.'

'No Fran, you won't. All we care about is that you get better, and we're so proud of the way you're soldiering on, but you need time to deal with this news. IBM will still be here tomorrow – don't worry – because worrying won't do you any good.'

John was an absolute gem, and concern like his helped me get through the worst times.

At the next consultation, my haematologist mentioned he had met the world's leading expert on Chronic Myeloid Leukaemia at a medical conference. The man's name was Professor Goldman, based at the Hammersmith Hospital in London. I asked whether I could get in touch with him, the haematologist offered to write a referral letter, and shortly afterwards I was offered an appointment.

So Adrian and I went to London. Until this time I'd had a series of unfortunate encounters with the medical profession. No specialist or nurse had ever said they were sorry for me, or reached out, even though I was reeling from shock and trauma. So my expectations of Professor Goldman weren't high.

And they sank to rock bottom as we waited in the Hammersmith for our appointment. We had to wait until the end of the session and assumed Professor Goldman always sees new patients after other appointments, so he could allocate them a longer time. We had to sit for over three hours in the busiest, hottest and dingiest waiting-room we'd seen yet. Some of the people waiting with us looked as though they didn't have long to live, which made me even more afraid.

I kept thinking, 'In a little while, that's going to be me.'

I have nothing but the highest praise for our National Health Service, it has saved my life, but there isn't any money to provide comfortable surroundings or a sense of well-being.

But Professor Goldman was wonderful, from the first moment we met him. He seemed a bit like a mad professor, fiercely intelligent and focused, quiet and unassuming despite his fame. He asked us so many questions and I sensed he understood and knew what we were going through. He was the first professional who made me feel he was sitting inside my skin and looking out. The facts he spelled out to us were not necessarily the things we wanted to hear, but information we badly needed.

At the end of the consultation we asked our page of pre-prepared questions. Adrian had begun keeping a notebook of every appointment and discussion, and he pencilled in the answers. Sometimes Professor Goldman answered straight away, but more often he stared into space, and I was thinking 'Is he going to answer? Has he heard? Should we repeat the question?'

I met him many times before I learned it's just a way he has, when he's very deep in thought, he mulls over carefully before giving an answer. If he doesn't know, he always says so, and I've learned that if he doesn't know, it's probably because medicine hasn't got that far yet.

We talked about *Interferon* and he felt less confident it could provide a cure than my haematologist had done. And we talked about the recent termination of my pregnancy. Professor Goldman hinted that perhaps it could have been avoided, but it was nothing more than a hint at that first meeting. I felt devastated and yet supported in a strange way, knowing this man shared my feeling about having a child, he wasn't a person who would force me to make impossible choices about lives.

I told him 'I need to know everything about CML, and explore the best available treatments, wherever they may be. I'm absolutely adamant I'm going to get through this.'

'Your determination will be key Fran, but you need to know that the statistics are against you, CML is unpredictable and there is a lot we don't understand about treating it,' he said. 'I'm very happy to refer you to the top people in the USA and Canada and I'll arrange appointments for you to explore the possible avenues out there.'

I summoned all my courage, 'I don't know what you're going to think, but for me the most important thing in the world is to have a child.'

'OK. Hhmmm.' Professor Goldman thought for a long time on that one. 'You probably know that one of the unfortunate side effects of a bone marrow transplant is to make you sterile, because it prevents the ovaries from producing viable eggs. I have another patient who feels like you and she's getting around the problem by storing an embryo before her transplant. We haven't implanted yet but I feel she has a very good chance of success. So that could be an option for you.'

'Can leukaemia be passed on to a child from the mother?'

'No way, absolutely not, it isn't hereditary so that's impossible.'

'I need you to understand how much I want a family.'

'If I asked you how badly you wanted a child on a scale of one to ten, what would you say?'

'Ten, ten.'

'I see.'

'If my only chance of having a family is before a transplant then I want a child now.'

Professor Goldman paused and stared right into my eyes, it was unnerving. 'Then I'm going to ask you some very difficult questions. One, how do you feel about it Adrian?'

'I'm one hundred per cent, totally committed to having a baby. We're not going to let leukaemia rule our lives, it's not going to rule us, we will rule it. We have to accommodate it for treatment and so on, but we won't let it affect our key life decisions. It's going to come second at all times.'

'Hhmm, that's a very positive, optimistic attitude, and I like it,' Professor Goldman replied, 'Question two, do you have any backup for childcare? Facing the hard reality, it's a possibility Adrian may have to bring up the baby alone, and that's very difficult for any man. So, do you have a close relationship with your parents, do they live nearby, would you have their support?'

I pictured my dear Mum and Dad and their unswerving loyalty, and knew I could answer this one. 'Adrian's parents live in Manchester and they're retired, wonderful, and we can count on their support. My parents live a few miles away and I'm certain they would look after the baby. Certain.'

'But would they be willing to care for it for several months during a transplant, and would they provide backup if you don't come through?'

'We'll ask them, but I'm sure they would,' I said.

'We won't rule it out then, I'll back you if that's your decision. You would have to come off all treatment to conceive, and I could only give you three months grace. If you didn't conceive in that time, I'm afraid you would have to be sensible and accept it. At that stage we'd have to think of storing some eggs.'

'Are you saying I can try?' My heart was leaping inside me and I was forcing myself not to build up my hopes, only to have them smashed again.

'If it means this much to you Fran, I'll back you. I'll give you three months.'

When we walked out of the long consultation I started to cry, 'We've got an ally now,' I sobbed.

Only days later I had an appointment with the haematologist. I blurted it out straight away, 'Professor Goldman says he'll back me to have a baby!'

'For goodness sake Fran, what are you saying? You can't possibly have a child while you're on *Interferon*.'

'I'm coming off it.'

'Don't be ridiculous.'

'This is my plan, I want to come off all treatment for three months, try to conceive, and then I'll have no treatment for the nine months of pregnancy.'

'Yes, you don't have to spell it out, I know you can't have treatment while you're pregnant. I've got morals myself you know.'

It was almost a row. But I had done it, I had gained the agreement I longed for more than life itself, I was allowed to try for a child.

Once we had been given the all clear, Adrian and I did a lot of serious talking about the future. My leukaemia changed our whole outlook on bringing a child into the world.

'We've got to be more sure than any other couple Fran, people are going to tell us it's irresponsible to have a child when you're so ill.'

I was much more optimistic now, 'But a lot of children have only one parent and anyway, I'm going to get through this,' I said.

'We both believe you're going to make it, but we've got to look at the worst scenario. The practical aspects of childcare, finance and more important, the effect on the baby if it lost its mum.'

I knew that in the end, it must be Adrian's decision, it would be supremely selfish of me to go ahead with a pregnancy if he wasn't absolutely committed. So I asked him the question neither of us wanted to face, 'Could you handle it if you were left on your own with our baby but without me?'

Adrian looked away for a second and stared into the distance. 'Yes Fran, the baby would be a living reminder of you, and I would absolutely love to bring up our child. But I don't want to think this way – it's such a negative thought – your illness is not a reason to abandon our plans for a family. I'm never giving up on you.'

I hugged him tight.

'But you'll have to be very brave if you get pregnant,' he said, 'a lot of people won't approve, and some medics will think we made the wrong choice.'

I never guessed how accurate Adrian's words would prove to be.

We drove to my parents immediately and dropped the bombshell. Mum was very quiet but Dad blurted out angrily, 'You're absolutely off your head Fran! As far as I'm concerned you're fighting for your life, and to add another complication is downright stupid!'

Mum leaped in, 'But if that's what you both want, Dad and I will back you.'

'No Avril, we won't. I'm absolutely flabbergasted and I don't think it's right. I just want to make sure Fran survives, and don't want them to bring in any complications which will affect that.'

Adrian put his finger to his lips to keep me quiet, 'The thing is, Professor Goldman says it can be done, albeit at a risk, but he wouldn't let Fran do something which put her life in further danger. The question we need to ask you both is, would you be prepared to look after the baby for a few months while Fran has her transplant, or to support me if I end up being a single father?'

Dad wouldn't look at me, but Mum moved forward and hugged Adrian, 'Yes, yes, of course we would, you don't even need to ask. I think it's wonderful news, and Dad will be fine when he's calmed down a bit.'

Dad didn't look as if he was calming down yet, but I totally understood where he was coming from. He just wanted me to survive, and to him a baby was tomorrow's problem. Looking back, my parents were pretty amazing, right at the point in their lives when they should have been settling down to enjoy retirement, I was asking them to take on a huge new responsibility of care and worry, and they rose to it with more love than any child deserves. I thank God I was that child.

My GP was wonderful about the news. He was really excited and said, 'I'll get you an appointment to see the consultant gynaecologist at Leamington, to advise you on pregnancy. Go into the waiting-room and I'll write to him immediately. If you've only got three months, you can't afford to wait for an appointment.'

I did as he asked, and a few minutes later Dr White reappeared waving a hand-written letter, 'I've phoned the hospital and if you go there straight away with this letter, Mr Hughes will see you. Good luck!'

I was staggered by his goodness.

It was yet another hospital, another depressing building. The Warneford Hospital in Leamington Spa was on the verge of being shut down, and it felt as though they had already given up on the place. I waited for ages, clutching the referral letter from my doctor, and panicking about meeting another big noise in the medical world.

But I needn't have worried. I was called in and after shaking my hand, Mr Hughes carefully read the letter from Dr White which was several pages long. I tried not to stare at him as he read. He was small, with a lovely round and smiley face and dark greying hair, I guessed his age as early fifties and watched him reading over the top of his half-moon spectacles.

I'll never, ever forget what happened next. He lifted his eyes from the last page, stood up and walked round to my chair. He put his hand out to me and said, 'You poor, poor girl. You've been through so much haven't you? We'll get you through, so don't worry.'

I felt tears welling up, no-one had been kind to me like this.

'I can tell how important it is to you to have a child, and I just hope you'll be successful. I can promise you my total support, I'll arrange fertility drugs to increase your chance of becoming pregnant quickly, and if you do conceive, I'll support you throughout pregnancy, and promise to be at the birth to make sure it goes well.'

I was overwhelmed by his kindness. From that day he became one of my favourite people, like an older uncle to a child, and he is now a very special friend. We had turned the corner.

It was September and my spirits began to lift for the first time since the spring. I felt elated by the chance I had been given, but terrified in equal measure, knowing how many women are unable to conceive, never mind in the space of three months! And as well as the pressure felt by any would-be mother, I was scared that my illness and all the treatments my body had been subjected to would prevent me conceiving. I pinned every hope and dream on a pregnancy, but dared not believe it would come true.

Adrian was adamant I needed to wind down after the emotional roller-coaster of the last six months, and shortly after I came off *Interferon*, we planned an exotic holiday to help me relax and improve my chance of becoming pregnant quickly.

At the end of November 1991, once my system was clear of *Interferon*, we took a last minute booking to Antigua to begin the period of three months' grace we'd been given by Professor Goldman.

On the outward flight we had several drinks, and I felt I was escaping from all the horror and craziness of the worst year of my life. Antigua was as beautiful and idyllic as I had always dreamed the Caribbean would be.

On that first evening, a steel band was playing Christmas carols, and Adrian and I walked hand in hand to the end of the pier, taking in the sheer beauty of the cool night air, the melody and the sea. The pier jutted right out into the water's edge and we sat with a glass of wine, talking more deeply than we had ever done about my condition. We spoke together of the future, our hopes and fears, and poured open our hearts.

I felt totally at peace, but unspeakably sad, overflowing with love for Adrian, but in despair that our happiness may be destroyed. It was one of the most bitter-sweet moments of my life.

We walked slowly back to our hotel room, and I am absolutely certain that was the night I conceived. It definitely wasn't the intention to get pregnant immediately, if that were the plan, we wouldn't have drunk so much wine!

The very next day Adrian and I were walking on the beach and a very strange thing happened. We were stopped by a woman who said, 'I'm a fortune-teller and I can tell your future.' She was a thin English woman who said she spent her summers in Antigua every year.

Adrian pulled me away, 'Come on Fran, don't get involved, I don't want you to talk to her.'

'Please let me, it can't do any harm, please Ade.'

'No way Fran, you only want to find out whether you're going to die, and I don't want you to hear anything bad. This is a stupid idea.'

But I begged him, I was desperate to talk to this thin, tanned woman who thought she could tell what would happen to me.

'You're carrying a child, and you have a child already,' she said.

'No, you're wrong, I don't have a child.'

'You have been pregnant before – you carried that child for a time – and you'll have two more children. One of them you're carrying here in Antigua.'

She insisted and scribbled her address down on a piece of paper, saying, 'When you go home you'll find out you're pregnant and I want you to write to me.'

It was very weird and she babbled on about a lot of other things which weren't true at all. I had an unpleasant feeling about the whole incident, although I was overcome by my fascination and a desire to believe her. The unpleasant feeling remained, and I never wrote to her when we returned home and wouldn't entertain the idea of seeking advice like hers again.

I had packed a pregnancy test in our holiday luggage and I did the first test before we left Antigua. The result showed positive, but I refused to believe it and as soon as we got home I bought another kit with a different brand. This time the display window turned a bright, clear pink. I simply couldn't believe what I saw and carried the plastic result tray around all day in my handbag, constantly checking the pink line to see whether it was still there.

I went straight to Dr White and asked him to do a pregnancy test.

He smiled at my keenness, 'These home kits are exactly the same as we use here Fran, but I know how much this means to you, and we'll test you anyway.'

When he got his result he smiled some more, 'Well you didn't waste any time did you?'

The funny thing was, I still had the fertility drugs prescribed by Mr Hughes, unopened and unused. I hadn't even needed them.

People who have warm friends
Are healthier than those with none.

A single real friend is a treasure
Worth more than gold or precious stones.

Anon.

Chapter Five

Chance in a Million

ೞ ೞ ೞ ೞ

So I was pregnant, and this time nobody was going to take my baby away. I would fight and win, whatever the cost to myself.

Although I had conceived, the search was going on to find a bone marrow donor who could save my life, a search that was all the more poignant now I was going to become a mother.

When I was first diagnosed, I'm not even sure I had heard of the charity The Anthony Nolan Bone Marrow Trust. But the story of a little boy who died from a bone marrow disease many years ago, triggered a bell in my distant memory. I learned that Anthony Nolan was the little boy who died tragically, after a fruitless search for a bone marrow donor. His mother's campaign to find a donor established the charity that now bears Anthony's name and has saved the lives of countless people. Although her efforts could not save her little boy, Shirley Nolan's tireless work has brought hope to thousands who came after her son.

Once my brother had been excluded as a possible donor for me, our haematologist had begun a correspondence with Anthony Nolan in the search for an outside donor. The process is slow and can be frustrating, but gives leukaemia sufferers the only real chance of a cure.

As usual, Adrian took control of the situation, and although the procedure for donor search is between the haematologist and Anthony Nolan, Adrian became close to the wonderful staff, especially Linda Hartwell with whom he was often in contact. She must have found him a pest, but they developed a genuine rapport.

Tests of all donors are done on a small blood sample and either the first four or all six antigens are processed and logged on to the Anthony Nolan database. Initially Anthony Nolan searches their database of donor bone marrow types looking for a match to the new patient. During the initial search, the patient's six antigens are compared with donors, and in more than half of cases there are a number of initial hits.

It was exciting when Adrian heard that at my first attempt there had been three hits. For some patients there will be many more, but in my case, as my antigens were unusual, the number of matches was always going to be low.

Once a hit has been established, Anthony Nolan can go on to do more detailed typing, which is necessary for a bone marrow transplant. With a sibling it's likely that several of the remaining antigens in your genetic code will also be identical, but when you test with a complete stranger that's very unlikely. So, Anthony Nolan is looking for a perfect six-antigen match to reduce the risk of rejection of the patient's body by the donor's immune system.

But searching for a full match is a complex and expensive procedure. Each donor who is a potential match must be recalled for a further blood test and each additional analysis costs Anthony Nolan fifty pounds per donor.

So although we were excited about the three possible matches, we knew it would be a long search. Each donor was recalled in turn and the analysis took several weeks. Many tests have to be done, including putting the blood of patient and donor together in a culture to watch the ensuing fight, which helps to predict the danger of rejection after transplant. This is known as Graft-versus-Host, and unlike an organ transplant, with bone marrow it is the new bone marrow and resultant immune system that rejects the patient's body, a potentially lethal problem.

On investigation, none of my three first hits proved to have the magic six antigen match. However, after several weeks, Anthony Nolan thought one of the three possible donors looked promising. At my next consultation with the haematologist I was hoping for good news.

Instead he said, 'The possible donor has decided to withdraw from the Anthony Nolan register, so that line of approach is closed.'

Immediately I crumpled and began to weep.

'Why are you crying?' the haematologist asked. 'You should be grateful that there's a register at all, and there are people who have volunteered to try to help you. You're being selfish and ungrateful – people go on the register out of goodwill and they have every right to withdraw if they want.'

It was too much for me. This was the man who had made me terminate my pregnancy, and who had never had a single supportive word for me. I finally flipped. I stood up and shouted 'I can't take your attitude any more, so piss off!'

I walked past Adrian, and out of the consulting room, slamming the door behind me.

Adrian apologised and told the haematologist we would be in touch, and then he drove me home.

I was hysterical, mortified by this medic who couldn't understand the blindingly obvious – that this news meant the difference between life and death. My form of leukaemia, CML, was fatal, and ten months earlier I'd been given five years to live. A transplant was my only chance, my brother had been excluded, and now there was nobody else to try. My last ray of hope had been extinguished and we had come to the end of the line, but he thought I was ungrateful and selfish to weep.

I remember Adrian speaking to my parents that evening who phoned eager to hear our news, and he told them he thought there was a personality clash with the haematologist. I heard him say 'He's not there for Fran and we'll have to find somebody else.'

Looking back now, I think the haematologist had a problem handling my emotion. Many of the decisions and events in those early days made me cry, and he couldn't cope with that. Maybe he thought I was a silly emotional female, and maybe he was the wrong man for me. All professionals have opinions, and his didn't match mine. But whatever the reasons, his attitude had made that first year even harder than it needed to be.

I talked to Adrian and we agreed I should go straight to Dr White and ask him to refer me to a different haematologist.

But as soon as I went into his consulting room I began to cry again. I was shaking in case he was angry with me, and I was nervous of criticising one of his colleagues. So I could hardly get the words out, 'I'm very grateful for all you've done for me ... I'm so worried ... what will you think of me?... I couldn't get on with him ... I'm truly sorry ...'

'Fran, Fran, it isn't a problem. I'm only sorry you've been upset. I'll get a referral letter off to the haematologist at Warwick Hospital straight away and it will all be sorted out.'

I blew my nose and looked at him with deep gratitude, feeling a weight lift from my shoulders at last.

The haematologist at Warwick was Dr Rose, who had given the original diagnosis of leukaemia and who had a gentle manner. To his immense credit, he never asked me about the conflict with his colleague, and he has supported me patiently now for ten years. I still see him to this day for my regular check-ups. He's kind and honest and always tells me what he would do if he were in my situation. And if he doesn't know an answer he says, 'You should ask that one to Professor Goldman!'

Dr Rose promised to be at the baby's birth, to take some cells from the umbilical cord. He told us about research suggesting that in a few cases, the cord blood cells can be used for a transplant to the mother. This technique had been successfully used in a transplant to a child with leukaemia when a younger brother was born, and Dr Rose didn't want us to miss this potential opportunity. The cells must be taken at the moment of birth, when they are immature, less aggressive than adult cells and not yet fully formed.

I was encouraged by this ray of hope and knew that if we failed to find a bone marrow donor, we had another possible avenue to explore.

So all my difficulties with the medical team were resolved, and that night Adrian and I wrote a letter together to the original haematologist explaining we were parting company. One year on from diagnosis we had a great team; a wonderful GP, a superb local haematologist and an international CML specialist. Whatever my outcome, I know now that when you're putting your life in the hands of other people, you need to trust and believe in them. Every part of the team needs to be right, because it takes your last ounce of courage and assurance for a transplant, as I came to know only too well. Although not everyone is referred to Professor Goldman directly, most CML cases are discussed with him by the consultant in charge, as my case still is to this day by Dr Rose.

If I was giving advice to anyone with a life-threatening condition it would be this: when you don't trust the advice you're being given, or when you don't feel supported, ask for help. Ask for a referral or for another opinion. All the best medics I have met are only too willing to seek extra help, and after all, your life may depend on it.

Although I was now a patient of Professor Goldman, and I had been told he was the world's leading expert for the treatment of Chronic Myeloid Leukaemia, there were yet more avenues of treatment to explore. Professor Goldman had already promised to arrange meetings with the experts in the United States and Canada, and at a consultation in 1992 he explained our options.

While I was struggling to find a bone marrow donor, research was being done in America on autologous transplants, as an alternative to using a donor. An autologous transplant carries much less risk to the patient because it involves the use of your own bone marrow, thus reducing the likelihood of rejection by your immune system. The transplant procedure is identical to a donor transplant, so the patient's body is exposed to total irradiation to kill the leukaemia, before the bone marrow is injected into your body. The only difference is that your own cleaned, screened bone marrow is injected back into your body, instead of a stranger's. At that time the leading international centre in research of autologous transplants was Vancouver in Canada.

Professor Goldman also told us about research in Seattle where the famous opera singer José Carreras had recently undergone a successful bone marrow transplant, and he thought I should explore their methods too.

We knew it would cost an arm and a leg to travel to America to talk to the consultants, but Adrian was adamant, 'We'll go and see these people and find out all the facts about the best chance of survival. Then we can make an informed decision about the way forward.'

We talked to my parents who thoroughly supported Professor Goldman's suggestions that I pursue every alternative, and they offered to fly to the States with us.

I was twenty weeks pregnant when we got on the plane, armed with letters of referral and notes from Professor Goldman for the American medics. This trip was before my pregnancy became public knowledge, and only close family knew the secret. Until then my tummy had remained pretty flat and I was hiding the small bump under a baggy jumper, but overnight, while we flew to Seattle, my clothes ceased to fit. I was uncomfortable throughout the flight and as we walked through customs I said to Adrian, 'I'm going to need some new clothes, I haven't packed a single maternity outfit!'

So the first thing we did on our medical fact-finding mission to the States, was go clothes shopping. This really pleased my husband and Dad! We hunted in every clothes shop in Seattle, but the only thing I could find that fitted and looked acceptable was a pair of denim maternity dungarees, which became my uniform for the next two weeks.

Our first appointment was at the Seattle private hospital, and I was totally shocked to see the contrast in facilities and surroundings between American hospitals and our own in Britain. There, evidence of money is all around you, and patients are treated as valued customers.

The transplant unit at the Fred Hutchinson Cancer Research Center couldn't have been more different to UK hospitals. The building looked like a brand new hotel, and Adrian said comparing Seattle to the Hammersmith was the difference between a palace and a garden shed. All the US hospitals we visited were spectacular, with fountains spouting in front, and made of new clean brick unlike the Hammersmith's red bricks blackened by years of dirt. In America the interior of the hospitals was spotless, brand new, immaculate and luxurious with thick deep carpets. It really opened up another world to us.

In the US it is medical policy that after bone marrow transplant the patient lives in an artificial bubble to ensure total protection from infection, bacteria and the normal environment. Hospital facilities in Seattle were state-of-the-art, and their standards of hygiene phenomenal.

Before my appointment with Dr Dean Buckner I was shown a video in the transplant unit that seriously frightened me, and forced me to face the realities of bone marrow transplant for the first time. In graphic detail the video showed the terrible things that are done to your body, and the potential side effects of Graft versus Host. I had never seen this level of detail about the medical procedure, and the realism of it terrified me.

As I watched the television monitor, I started to sweat and shake, and had an overwhelming desire to run away from the hospital. The battle of emotions inside me was as unpleasant as the video, I was fighting between the desire to hide from the truth, and a desperate longing to live for the sake of my unborn child. A new anger and bitterness about my illness welled up and spilled over as tears. And yet I knew a transplant, just like the horrible ones shown in the video, was my only possibility of hope.

When we met Dr Buckner he was a genuine and honest guy who fully understood why I had decided to get pregnant before treatment for the leukaemia, and he wished me the best luck in the world. He was very straightforward about the Seattle clinic and set out its strengths and limitations for us.

At last I said, 'I'm asking you to be completely honest, if you were in my shoes, what would you do?'

His answer really shocked me. 'I'll be delighted to take you on here as my patient and we can promise to do our utmost to help, but Professor Goldman is the best in the world for CML, he really is the top guy. You couldn't beat him.'

'But our facilities in the UK are nothing like yours, our hospitals don't have enough money.'

'Your National Health Service is the envy of the world Fran, and the most important thing is to have the right consultant, irrespective of the surroundings.'

I looked around at the immaculate consulting room and thought of the spotless wards and hi-tech facilities we had seen here, and I found it hard to take in his words. This American medic was recommending Professor Goldman who worked in such a different and inferior environment.

'At the end of the day Fran,' he said, 'we've got all the facilities here, but Professor Goldman has a special instinct and knowledge, and you can't put a price on that.'

As we drove back to the motel, the four of us mulled over what had been said.

'There would be so much to think about if you decided to be treated out here,' said Dad, practical as ever. 'We would have to book into a hotel so we could be near you during your recovery, and we'd have to live out here for several months, maybe longer. There's no way you'd be allowed to fly home to England until you had the all clear from the hospital. It's feasible, but would take a lot of planning.'

'But I must stand a better chance of survival here with such fantastic facilities,' I protested, 'a transplant is a transplant, but the biggest danger is what happens to you afterwards. There would be no chance of infection in the Seattle hospital.'

But I knew my recovery could take more than a few months. And by then we would have a child. It was going to be a big decision.

We drove to Vancouver in Canada to meet the leading expert on autologous transplants.

While I sat in the waiting room before my appointment, I leafed through the binders of information about leukaemia. Again, here was more detail than I had ever been given about the true horrors of a transplant. I was reading facts I didn't want to believe, about terrible side effects, and getting more and more angry about the unfairness of it all. The struggle went on inside me and I was shocked and frightened by what I read.

Dr Mike Barnett was as kind and warm as the man in Seattle. He gave in-depth, clear answers to all of my questions and explained that autologous transplants were still in their infancy. They weren't a miracle cure, or even a certain one.

He too was prepared to take me on, 'But you're from the best country in the world to have leukaemia,' he said.

'What do you mean?'

'Because it's where Professor Goldman works – you'd be in the safest hands with him. I know we're the international centre of competence for autologous transplants, but the bottom line is that Professor Goldman is highly revered here. Whenever he's speaking at a medical conference we all try to go and hear him. There are plenty of

CML consultants around the world, and they're excellent medics, but Goldman is the key guy in the business.'

This was the most comforting news I could ever hear. The trip to America had cost a fortune, but it was worth every penny for the peace of mind it brought.

I came out of the appointment in Vancouver and we went for a family coffee in a local shopping mall. As soon as we sat down at the table I said to Adrian and my parents, 'Professor Goldman will do my transplant, and I won't go anywhere else.'

The faith expressed in him by these other highly qualified medics meant everything to me. When you put your life into the hands of another human being, you need to trust that person absolutely, and now I could.

'Good, now we can go for it,' said Adrian.

'So what are you going to call this baby?' asked Mum.

We sat, expectant mother, husband and grand-parents-to-be, and discussed all the nicest and silliest names we could think of. We giggled and released the tension that had been building throughout the trip.

I was sure the baby would be a boy, and someone suggested the name Matthew. I said, 'I really like that – unless something else comes to us – I think it will be Matthew.'

We were worn out by travelling and the stress of weighing up the information we had been given. But I had made my decision, and before we flew home, we agreed to take a few days holiday on the coast. The rest and relaxation did me a power of good, and my spirits lifted another degree.

I lay on a sun-lounger by the hotel pool and thought everything through, the commitment to Professor Goldman, and my fear of the Hammersmith Hospital. Maybe some people like to shut out the potential dangers, but I need to examine and face them. So I lay in the warm sun, contemplating all the horrors I had seen in the video and hospital binders, and turned each fact over in my mind. I considered the worst possible outcome, and the worst side-effects, preparing myself and planning for them. In my experience, nothing seems so bad once you have examined it and talked it though with yourself.

And as I lay there, I prayed, for myself and our baby, and I took comfort from the certain knowledge that other people were praying for me too, and that certainty supported me in the darkest hours. People wrote to say they had lit candles for me in cathedrals, and one whole church congregation was praying for me.

Once we arrived home I looked very pregnant and knew I must take the plunge and announce it at work on my first day back. My manager and colleagues were delighted and supportive, although they must have thought we were taking a crazy risk. One of the lads said 'I wondered why you had stopped wearing your slick business suits and started coming to work in baggy jumpers!'

That night I looked up some of the baby names we had discussed in a book of names. When I turned to 'M' I read, 'Matthew means a gift from God.' I called to Adrian, 'Gordon Bennett! That's it Adrian, our baby is going to be called Matthew.' I was amazed that we had chosen the right name so light-heartedly, before we knew why it was perfect.

So I was half way through pregnancy and no suitable donor had been traced for me. The growing baby inside focussed my mind on survival, and I determined to do something positive.

One evening Adrian and I sat down and talked about the need for a donor. I felt despondent and hopeless, knowing my antigen type was rare. 'What if I never find a donor?' I asked him.

'You will find a donor, I have no doubt of that Fran, there's someone out there for you, and finding them is just a numbers game.'

'But it's much harder for me than a patient who has a common antigen type.'

'So we get more people through the door, until the right one is found. We'll raise awareness and raise money until we find that donor.'

We told colleagues at IBM that we needed to encourage more people to volunteer as bone marrow donors, and to our amazement everybody rallied round. IBM went to town and set up a 'Chance in a Million' campaign to raise awareness and funds for The Anthony Nolan Bone Marrow Trust.

Ever since I first came across the charity, it seemed to be unique. There are many organisations that do wonderful work in research and support those with serious illness, but Anthony Nolan is the only charity I know which offers patients a cure. The administration of the donor register is the last life-line for people like me, and that makes Anthony Nolan very special.

Chance in a Million began with the few people who worked in our IBM branch, but the news of my condition soon spread, until the whole company of twenty thousand employees was on board. Everybody wanted to help, and I was overwhelmed by the wave of support and kindness I felt. It was a very humbling experience, and the power of affection buoyed me up more than I can ever explain.

Adrian gave briefings to staff saying, 'It's very hard to accept there isn't a donor for Fran yet, and we need to appeal for new donors. And every time someone signs up, we may be helping someone else on the Anthony Nolan register get a transplant.'

The IBM management took it all very seriously and decided to set up a committee. Before long, Chance in a Million was a national organisation, represented by most IBM sites. The committee set targets to raise £50,000 and get 2,500 new donors on the register, and they attacked the project with all the gusto of marketeers and professional sales-people.

Staff at my own site in IBM Warwick were absolutely fantastic. Immediately they planned a local donor day and liaised with Anthony Nolan to be on hand to receive donors.

It was a huge success, and many new donors gave blood samples and volunteered to go on the register that day. That was when we first met Marjorie Gordon-Box of Anthony Nolan who helped us to arrange all donor sessions, and she became a key person later in our story.

In the middle of all the excitement, an IBM receptionist contacted me and said there was a press photographer asking to take a photo of me. I assumed someone must have called the local paper to help us with publicity, so I agreed to go outside with Adrian for a few pictures. Only seconds after meeting the photographer, he picked up on the fact that I was pregnant and waiting for a transplant, and said he would like to put our picture in the local press, such as the *Leamington Courier*. I agreed, hoping it would help raise local support.

I gave no more thought to the publicity, and it never crossed my mind I would hear from the press again. But if I had known what that single photo would lead to, I would have thought twice before trundling to reception.

Within days, from that one short photo session, an avalanche of media interest descended on me. Suddenly I was inundated with calls from the press, local photographers, journalists and even television researchers. I fielded as much attention as I could, and asked them to focus on the Chance in a Million campaign. I had no desire to be in the papers, but could see the potential benefits of raising public awareness of the need for donors. Again, I hoped the attention would die down, and did my best to forget about it.

After the success of the donor day, IBM Warwick ran a Valentine's ball, and then came up with the idea of a sponsored bike ride, from the most northerly IBM site to the most southerly, cycling the entire distance, and throwing a donor day at every stop. Each site arranged a local co-ordinator, who I feared must be thoroughly cheesed off with the extra workload, but nobody complained. Avis donated a hire car for me to travel in, and several large hotels across Britain offered free accommodation and meals to the team for the overnight stops, and we were thrilled when Terry Butcher, the former England football captain, agreed to cycle with us. His support proved vital in raising the profile of the event.

The cyclists included Terry, my brother Nick and poor Adrian who threw himself into training with the fiery spirit that had never dwindled. But the most remarkable member of the team was one of my own customers, Tony Hubbard of GEC Alsthom. I had explained to all my customers that I had leukaemia, feeling very embarrassed and unprofessional to admit it, and when Tony heard about the bike ride he announced he loved cycling. 'Hang on a minute Fran, can I join the team?' he asked.

'But you're a customer, I'm your SE!' I said.

'Is that a problem? Ask your boss, I'd love to do this for you.'

IBM were delighted that a key customer felt happy to be involved, and GEC managers were fantastic. They gave Tony time off work for the bike ride and rallied round him in support, and so he joined us.

With newspaper headlines like 'Butcher's on his bike again!' the boys pedalled from Greenock in Scotland to IBM's head office in Portsmouth. When they came through IBM Warwick, the place went wild and we had hot air balloons, and huge public enthusiasm. One of the most moving moments of my life happened that day. I had got to know Bob Brolley, a DJ on Coventry radio through the IBM fund-raising campaign, and he had always been absolutely wonderful to us, even giving me his silver crucifix which meant a lot to him, hoping it would bring me blessings. Several times I had been invited to speak on his radio show, and when the IBM bike ride came to Warwick, Bob took over the IBM clubhouse and transmitted a live broadcast from there.

When the cyclists arrived, they pedalled to the club-house and I rushed up to Bob to give him a hug, but he looked drawn and tired.

'How are you Bob?'

'I'm OK, but yesterday my brother was in a serious road accident and he's critically ill, it's touch and go. I was with him last night.'

'Why are you still here?'

'Because I want to help you Fran.'

The breath went right out of me and I stood and looked at this wonderful man who was soldiering on for my sake, despite a personal tragedy. I gave his cross back to him and prayed his brother would be all right. I was touched to the core and realised that receiving love is more important than raising funds.

But the bike ride was a resounding money raiser too, Gary Lineker and Brian Robson lent their support to the campaign, and by the time we reached Portsmouth we had raised £30,000 and a thousand new donors.

There were a few mess-ups along the way, and it was a stressful, tiring time, and I don't know how I managed to cope with the inevitable strain of being thirty-four weeks pregnant and with leukaemia, but the support of everybody we met kept me going.

A few days after the bike ride, Adrian was surprised to have a phone call from Tony Hubbard, my customer at GEC. 'Excuse me Adrian, but can you tell me the name of the IBM girl we met at the Manchester donor event, because she was absolutely gorgeous?'

'Aye aye,' said Adrian, 'she's Jules and I'll get in touch for you.'

On the very same day, I had a call from Jules in IBM Manchester, 'Fran – what's the name of that guy who cycled with Adrian – he was fantastic!'

Adrian and I laughed about it that night, but Tony did ask Jules out and later married her, and we are now godparents to their two children. All of that happiness began because of my leukaemia.

Many friends and strangers performed amazing acts of support. Ansy, a school friend who is now a professional singer, persuaded a friend to cycle with her from Land's End to John o'Groats, staying with local churches every forty or sixty miles, and performing a concert at each venue. The biggest was in Warwick, and hundreds of people crammed into the church to hear an evening of quite superb opera and popular music. It was a profoundly moving occasion (and an amazing total was raised).

That June the Warwickshire police force ran their annual gala day to raise money for charity. We were thrilled when a local Sergeant, Richard Woodcock, offered to support my cause as part of the gala. He arranged for Anthony Nolan to attend and take blood samples from police staff and the public, and on a hot summer day, dozens of people queued to join the list of donors. At least two hundred new donors were signed up on that day alone.

I was bowled over by the support, but taken aback when the police asked me to go to the tannoy at the end of the gala and make a speech. This was the first time I had been asked to speak to a huge crowd, and I was absolutely terrified. I'm naturally quiet and hate to be the centre of attention, but I summoned up everything I could remember from my IBM training in presentation skills, and stumbled to the microphone.

I've no idea what I said, but managed to string some words together, and told the crowd how much their support meant to me. It was really difficult, but now I'm glad I gained the confidence to speak in public, and know I have helped to raise awareness for Anthony Nolan this way.

Other companies who ran superb donor days included Carr's Paper, Millward Brown, the National Grid and Peugeot. The IBM salesman to Peugeot suggested a donor day, and the local TV channel covered their amazing donor event. When the factory siren rang out for break, the entire production line down-tooled and formed a queue to donate blood to join the donor register.

Then a friend whose family are connected with toll bridges arranged for a Saturday gift day when the entire road-bridge toll would be given to Anthony Nolan. When Adrian and I arrived by car, our friends Pete and Richard leaped out at us dressed in full Highwayman regalia, even carrying toy guns. We laughed all day watching them do the same to innocent drivers, who threw far more than the toll fee into the buckets. A lot of money was raised that day.

My initial motivation in all the work we started for Anthony Nolan was of course personal. I had a vested interest in increasing the number of donors on the register, but it quickly became something much less self-centred. The charity work gave me an enormous sense of purpose, and I loved every minute of it. Although I dreaded public attention, I relished the effect my story was having, and I have learned the truth that in doing something for others, you receive blessings a hundred-fold.

For years afterwards IBM colleagues and strangers told Adrian they had been selected to be bone marrow donors. And even to this day Anthony Nolan staff phone me and say, 'You'll never guess what! We've just had another successful donor match and the donor says he volunteered because of you.'

Sometimes it can be traced back to the IBM connection, sometimes to the media coverage of my story. I don't know the donors, but I feel an immense joy and gratitude when I hear someone else's life has been saved because of the support people gave to me. It's one of the wonderful blessings which has come out of my suffering – who says every cloud doesn't have a silver lining!

Chapter Six

Matthew

附 ᔆ ᔆ ᔆ

My pregnancy progressed smoothly, although at times my life became unbearable. The trouble began with the single photo session I had at the first IBM donor day.

After the initial flurry of local media interest, the press excitement had died down, and I breathed a huge sigh of relief. But a few days before my thirtieth birthday in July 1992, I was contacted by a researcher from a national newspaper. They wanted to take a few pictures of me at home with Adrian for a short newspaper piece on my story.

At first I fielded the request and said I had no interest in further publicity. I had just finished work at IBM and was winding down for the last few weeks of pregnancy. But the researcher was insistent, and played on the benefits of national publicity for raising awareness of leukaemia and attracting donors.

Maybe I was a fool, but I warily agreed to a photo-shoot at our home. Only hours later, a photographer and journalist called and took a series of pictures of Adrian and I, holding a fluffy white teddy bear, sitting on the lawn in various poses, and standing together with Adrian cradling my bump.

The blonde journalist was quiet, very friendly and understanding, and I spoke to her relatively freely about our hopes, dreams and fears. She was Pat Tracey working with her freelance photographer son Danny, and we liked them both.

Within days, my story exploded across the national press. The *Daily Star, Daily Mail, Today, Daily Express* and *London Evening Standard* were the first papers to run the story. In my innocence I had no idea how journalists sell and borrow stories from one another, and I had not anticipated the spin that would be put on my words.

Suddenly I was transformed by the media into a brave but desperate dying woman who was on the verge of delivering a baby with her last gasp.

I was very pleased to be raising the profile of Anthony Nolan and the issue of the international donor shortage, and I knew the phrase 'all publicity is good publicity', but felt the situation was getting out of hand.

I quickly learned that one picture and one article are never enough for the papers. After the first rush of articles, the phone was red hot with journalists, photographers and agents ringing to ask for more pictures and interviews. I stopped answering the phone, then pulled the cord out of its socket to give myself some peace. Adrian became really angry, because he was out at work all day and wasn't able to protect me from the barrage of intrusion. A close friend recommended an answer machine to intercept our phone calls which made a huge difference to our quality of life.

The birth date was looming and the obvious danger to me provided the media with a big human interest story. My family and friends began to get upset, and my brother Nick was appalled to open the paper on his way home from work one evening and read the headline 'Will having a baby cost Fran her life?'

Then we had a call from Pat Tracey who asked whether we would like her to act on our behalf and filter all media approaches. Adrian felt this would be a good way of taking control of the situation, Pat knew our terms, that we wouldn't agree to interviews or pictures unless the newspaper printed contact details for Anthony Nolan with information on how to become a donor. At least this way we felt the media coverage could have a purpose.

Having Pat on our side made an enormous difference, but the attention still had a degree of control over our lives. I did interviews only to discover that when the article appeared, I was quoted as saying things that were wildly off the mark. The journalists assumed I wouldn't live to see my child's first birthday, or first day at school, and I found these remarks desperately difficult and hurtful. While I was trying so hard to be positive for myself, the newspapers wanted to hook their readers' emotions.

I'm not criticising or complaining, and I'll always be grateful for the press coverage that led to new donors and lives of other people being saved, but it would be a lie to say this was an easy time. And I understand media spin, how a story is designed to tug at readers' heart-strings – the trouble was – each story tugged at mine. Of all the news angles, one hurt me more than any other, the prediction that I wouldn't live to take my child to school. At the centre of this and every story was the hard-line core – that I probably wouldn't survive. And I had to read these words just when I most needed super-human faith and determination to live for my family.

As the birth of our baby approached, I wanted to prepare and relax and enjoy the last few weeks, but with one exception, that didn't happen.

That oasis was my thirtieth birthday, three weeks before my due date. Adrian had arranged to take me to *Charingworth Manor* in the Cotswolds for a surprise dinner with our four parents, my brother and his wife.

I had no idea that anyone else was joining us for dinner, and when Adrian led me into the intimate dining room overlooking the beautiful English country garden, the happiness of the surprise took my breath away. It was mid July, and the french windows were open onto rose bushes in full bloom, where bees hummed amongst the evening lavender.

I looked at the circle of smiling faces, my Mum, brother and family, and overflowed with love for them all. How I wanted to spare them from the pain of my leukaemia, and the worry of the coming birth!

There were tears of joy in my eyes as I sat down at the table, and a few minutes passed before I noticed a small box in the centre of my cream dinner plate.

I looked at Adrian and he was smiling. The expression in his face was pure love.

Inside the box, nestling in dark velvet, was the most beautiful eternity ring I have ever seen.

'I love you,' he whispered, 'for ever Fran.'

It was one of the most romantic moments of my life, and I know that in a strange way the leukaemia has made those moments deeply poignant and precious. Maybe we don't value our blessings until we're in danger of losing them.

Later he told me he had the ring made with the intention of giving it to me at the baby's birth, but he was so scared by the huge wall of uncertainty ahead, he decided to give it to me early.

He didn't say the words, but I knew his unspoken dread, I might not make it. At the pit of my stomach I acknowledged the gnawing monster of fear.

Perhaps it seems odd , but it was only towards the end of pregnancy that I worried significantly about the awful possibility something could go wrong. In the early months I was wrapped up in the joy of falling pregnant so quickly, and by the drive of fund-raising.

I had been remarkably well and my white blood cell count rose throughout pregnancy at a gradual pace, but towards the end I became very frightened when I worked out the potential top limit. I kept doing calculations to work out how high the count would go by the full term of nine months.

At the very end of the pregnancy my count was climbing fast, reaching figures topping one hundred, when normal levels are as low as ten or twelve. The Hammersmith carried out filtration to reduce the white cell levels, a process that was to become a way of life for the next two years.

The medical team made detailed plans for the birth. I was really keen to have a natural labour with as little intervention as possible, and Dr Rose the haematologist agreed to let nature take its course. But he and an assistant haematologist were on call for whatever time labour began, and would attend the birth with facilities for harvesting cells from the umbilical cord. Dr Rose had prepared to harvest the blood cells and rush them into cold storage for a possible future transplant. Although the technology for this treatment was still in its infancy, we were hoping that in the absence of a donor match, or a failed transplant, the technology may have moved on far enough for me to try a future bone marrow transplant from the baby's cells. I was just glad Dr Rose would be there, in case I had a haemorrhage.

Professor Goldman had given us his home telephone number and would be on standby in case anything went wrong and he was needed to resolve an emergency. This was both comforting and terrifying at the same time, because it proved no-one was certain of success.

Every day during the last week of pregnancy I had phone calls from the media, desperate to know whether I had any signs of labour, each paper wanting to be first to run the story. We decided to keep things hush-hush, and warned the hospital in advance that there may be press intrusion. Staff were wonderfully supportive, and as the maternity ward was on the ground floor, they booked an upstairs room for me where I would be safe from photographers peeping through the windows.

I was so nervous about the birth that I had bought absolutely nothing for the baby during pregnancy. We had ordered the large goods like a pram, but hadn't taken delivery on a single item, because I didn't want to make any assumptions. We decorated the nursery in soft neutral colours, and there were no hints of the much-wanted baby in the room before the birth.

My due date was 7th August, and four days beforehand I bought a brown wicker chair for the nursery. It was my first and only purchase for the baby, but in my fearful state I told myself it would always be useful as a spare for the living room. If anything went wrong. When I got the chair home, I dragged it up to the nursery and set it proudly against the pastel green wall. I stood back to admire the chair and thought, 'That would look really good if it was white!'

My due date came and went, and in frustration I found a pot of Adrian's white gloss and set to work with a paint brush, hoping the exertion would trigger labour.

It must have worked, because the very next morning, on 10th August, I woke with sharp pains in my back and stomach. I prodded Adrian and said, 'I'm convinced I'm having contractions.'

'Hhhmm?' asked Adrian sleepily, 'but you don't seem to be in much pain,' and he rolled over again.

'Well they're only mild but I'm sure it is labour.'

The alarm clock went off shrilly.

'I'll take the day off work then,' yawned Adrian. A few moments later he jumped out of bed, 'I'll get your TENS machine – maybe you're in labour!'

'That's what I said!'

He connected me up to the mobile TENS machine lent by the hospital which generates a mild electric current to help manage the pain of contractions. After breakfast we took a short walk to the village green, because the midwife had told us gentle exercise can speed up labour. Every couple of minutes I had to stop and lean on Adrian's arm, saying, 'Oooh dear, oh my goodness!'

I stayed in the lounge all morning with the TENS machine for company, while Adrian pottered in the garden.

Every few minutes he leapt through the patio doors saying anxiously, 'Are you OK? Do you think we should go into hospital yet?'

'No, I want to delay it as long as possible, and stay at home until we absolutely have to go in.' I knew I would be much more relaxed at home than in hospital.

At six o'clock in the evening we rang the Warneford hospital and asked for advice. We explained the timing of contractions and they agreed I still had a long way to go.

'But as it's you Fran, it's probably a good idea for you to pack a bag, have a bath and come in this evening. We'd rather keep an eye on you.'

So that's what we did.

Once in hospital things began to speed up, but progress was still excruciatingly slow. My cervix refused to dilate, and the longer it went on, the more the baby's heart-beat dipped. We anxiously watched it on the monitor attached to my tummy, and the midwife had identified the baby was lying with its back against my spine which can make birth difficult, and I knew I was struggling.

So many people were standing round my bed, the midwife, paediatrician, Mr Hughes the gynaecologist, his assistant and Adrian, and it was obvious everybody was worried.

I heard Mr Hughes talking to Adrian, and then the midwife called, 'The heart beat has slowed almost to a stop, I don't like it.'

Mr Hughes spoke to Adrian in his gentle father-like manner, and then Ade leaned over me and said, 'Fran, Mr Hughes suggests you have a caesarean, the baby isn't happy and we don't want to take any risks. Is that OK?'

'Yes, yes,' I said. Suddenly the pain and worry were too much to bear, 'please help my baby and do whatever you have to. Just get the baby out please.'

'We'll have to perform the caesarean under general anaesthetic, because your high white cell count makes an epidural too risky. OK?'

Adrian soothed me and stroked my wet hair, 'It's the right decision Fran, you've been through so much and you gave it your best shot.'

The next thing I remember was waking up from the anaesthetic in the recovery room. I was drifting in and out of consciousness, and a nurse lifted a perfect, beautiful baby onto my chest.

Adrian was crouching beside me and tears were streaming down his cheeks, 'We've got a son Fran, and you're fine,' were the only words he could manage through his tears.

I looked down at the pink, creased body and I was filled to the fullness with a love I have never known. Our son was absolutely perfect, healthy, beautiful. It was without doubt the greatest moment of my life.

When we had been settled on the ward, one of the nurses asked, 'Any ideas for a name?'

I turned to her and answered with absolute certainty, 'His name is Matthew, because it means "A gift from God".'

It was several days before I accepted that Matthew was here to stay, and I think many mothers feel that way after their first birth. I lay for hour after hour just staring at our son in his perspex cot beside my bed, examining his tiny arms and fingers and ears with fascination. Every time he moved, my stomach turned over with joy and relief, I could see he was one hundred per cent normal. Part of me had spent the last nine months fearing my leukaemia may damage him, even though I knew this was medical nonsense. I can't express the relief and thankfulness I felt at seeing him perfect.

I remember ringing my Dad from the maternity ward and telling him, 'I know everyone says their baby is beautiful, but he absolutely, truly is, I'm not lying Dad.'

Even now when I look at the earliest photos taken of Matthew I am staggered by the unusual serenity in his face, God sent us a true miracle after all our suffering and fear.

I said very little to anyone in those first few days, even to Adrian, and I just wanted to lie and look at Matthew, enjoying the wonder of it all. We had crossed the most important hurdle and had a child, and I felt a surge of hope in knowing my story had departed from the script I feared. Maybe it wouldn't end like *Love Story* after all.

We now had a baby, but nothing at all for him to wear, sleep in or empty his bladder in! So on the day Matthew was born, Adrian rushed into Leamington with a long shopping list of essentials, and a note to collect the pram, cot and ordered items. At the same time my mother went to buy the things I didn't trust Adrian with, including baby-grows, vests and nappies.

Mum was quite bothered by my decision to wait before buying any clothes, 'You poor little mite!' she coo'ed at Matthew, 'you haven't a stitch to wear – Grandma will soon sort you out.'

Before I came home, Mum and Adrian turned the bland pastel bedroom into a nursery, putting up pictures, installing the cradle borrowed from my brother, and ordering a nappy changing unit. And now I knew my freshly painted wicker chair could be used for its true purpose, for nursing and feeding our child.

I stayed in hospital for five days and throughout my stay the press continued to ring up and bother the maternity staff for news and information. The reporters begged for a photo session so they could run a feature on the successful birth. They also asked permission to be on our driveway when we arrived home for the first time with Matthew, and we said 'No, no way!' to every request. We wanted the home-coming to be special and very private.

But Adrian felt sure that if we agreed to cooperate, the initial interest would die down and we would be given some peace. On our behalf, Pat Tracey rang the *Mirror*, who had been very supportive, and agreed to a photo session in hospital. The pictures taken by Pat and her son Danny were really beautiful and remain among my favourites of Matthew. I look tired but overjoyed, and Adrian just looks on top of the world.

The *Mirror* ran our story as a centre-page spread and front page. That day I spoke to my university flatmates to thank them for a beautiful bouquet of flowers, and they were shrieking down the phone as they pored over the *Sunday Mirror*. 'We're so excited Fran, we can't believe it's really you!'

I felt acutely embarrassed, and longed to be a normal new mum.

My emotions were all over the place, and I was still afraid there may be a photographer on our drive when we pulled up, but I needn't have worried. Adrian drove his new family with pride, and the homecoming with our miracle baby was an utterly special occasion. I remember looking up at the horse chestnut trees, dressed now in the deep green of high summer, and remembering the very different emotions with which I'd seen them fifteen months earlier. We had come a million miles since then.

Matthew went straight into his new nursery and we had a baby listening monitor in our bedroom. People have asked whether my illness made me a paranoid mother, but I honestly had no fear for him once he arrived. I had complete peace about Matthew, but not about myself.

On our first night at home with Matthew, we were sitting in bed watching the ITN *News at Ten*. Just before the commercial break we were stupefied to see the picture of me taken in hospital and heard the news reader trailer the item as a mum who had risked her life to have a miracle baby. Adrian leaped out of bed and hurtled downstairs to set the video recorder and came back to bed to watch the item. We sat in strange silence while our wonderful news was broadcast to the nation. I had absolutely no idea how the story had reached ITN, maybe the *Mirror* newspaper had passed it on. It felt so weird, and was a reminder that my life was far from normal, even now.

At this time my Dad rang me over breakfast and read out an article from his *Daily Telegraph* about Matthew's birth. Until then our story had been covered by the tabloids rather than broad-sheets and I was very shocked by the article appearing there.

It was hard to get much rest between feeds because the phone wouldn't stop ringing. I was very emotional in the first few days at home, and I found the media interest added to my exhaustion. The doctors had warned me that leukaemia would increase the post-natal tiredness felt by any new mother, and I yearned for a time of stillness and rest so I could take everything in. It may sound silly, but I began to worry about the many things that had been reported about my future, especially the idea I may not live to take Matthew to school. I actually felt more afraid now he existed and needed me.

At a weak moment when Adrian was out, I agreed to a TV session for GMTV, even though Matthew was less than three weeks old. I was still tugged by the hope that publicity would increase the number of bone marrow donors, and therefore my chance of finding a donor match.

GMTV sent a chauffeur-driven car to collect us and we were driven to Birmingham early on the morning of the show. We would be linked up to the GMTV studios in London by satellite for a live link, and before we went on air we were made-up and researchers gave us a pep talk about the questions we would be asked by Mike Morris.

The questions sounded perfectly reasonable, and we had no reservations. We were ushered into the studio and Mike talked to us off-air through ear-pieces to confirm the questions he would ask. We were both nervous when Mike began the live interview, but he didn't ask any of the prepared questions, and everything he said was a total shock.

The last question was the worst. Although the general tone of the short interview had been negative, right at the end Mike said, 'So Adrian, how do you think you'll cope as a single parent bringing little Matthew up?'

I was dumb-founded and thought 'What a question!' My eyes started to well up.

I could see Adrian was reeling from shock, but his answer was absolutely wonderful. He turned it around and said, 'That's a pointless and negative question because it isn't going to happen. Fran and I wouldn't have come this far if we intended to give up, and we have no intention of wasting energy on negative thoughts. We talked all this through before we decided to have a family. We don't need to go over it again now and make it sound as if we've written off the future. Fran and I will never give up.'

We had hoped the interview would be up-beat and positive, but instead it had looked into the future and assumed the worst. Both of us felt let down and regretted doing the interview, and although the media coverage did encourage new donors, we hated being in the spotlight and found the handling of us overbearing. I hope this book will answer many of the questions we've been asked in the past ten years, and also help other people who find themselves in the glare of publicity as we did.

But the media coverage brought huge blessings as well as pain. Only a few days after I gave birth came one of the most touching moments of my entire illness. Bob Brolley – the local DJ from Coventry Radio – set up his Saturday radio programme in support of me, and it was a very humbling experience. We had taken part in several earlier programmes, but the show he did when Matthew was new-born was by far the most special. Bob set up transmission with a make-shift clinic in a shop doorway in Coventry city centre, and broadcast an appeal for new donors to come and sign up with Anthony Nolan.

I was still in hospital and unable to be there in person, but my parents went to the busy shopping centre in my place. Mum told me the sight they saw brought tears to her eyes, but more amazingly to my Dad's too.

There was an enormous queue of people snaking from the shop doorway, right out of the shopping centre, lining up to become bone marrow donors. They were just ordinary people, mums and dads with kids in push-chairs, shoppers, skinheads with multiple earrings, young women and middle-aged men, black and white. Every one of them was giving up a Saturday to queue in the hot sun to register to offer to save someone's life. I wept when I heard, and was full of love for these good people, and can't deny I hoped one of them might be able to save me.

Blessings like that came to pass only because of our suffering, and they will never, ever be forgotten. Thank you from the bottom of my heart.

Chapter Seven

Katherine

ೞ ೲ ೞ ೲ

Adrian had many shocks in the course of my illness, and I think I gave him the biggest one of all with the bombshell I dropped on the day Matthew was born.

When he came back from essential baby shopping in the afternoon, he found me lying peacefully in the hospital bed.

I motioned to the chair, 'Sit down Ade, because I've got something very important to say.'

He put the carrier bags down on the floor, 'Whatever it is Fran, don't upset yourself.'

'I won't, it's something very positive. I've decided I want us to have another baby.'

Adrian ran his fingers through his hair, making it stand on end.

'Can we have another baby Adrian, this means everything to me?'

'Yes, fine, we'll think about it,' he said closing the subject.

I said nothing else that day and I knew he had stalled for time, but I held the decision rock-solid in the back of my mind. I'm a Bevan by birth and we're a bit like super-tankers, once we've set our minds on something it's almost impossible to turn us around. Call it stubbornness, call it determination, but we know our minds.

I didn't say a word to anyone else, but asked Adrian if we could raise the subject with Professor Goldman at my next appointment at the Hammersmith.

Once we were at home after the birth, several weeks passed before I was well enough to travel to London. But eventually my white cell count reached high levels and Dr Rose my haematologist said I had no choice but to make the journey.

I wasn't giving the medics an easy time, because I had insisted on delaying further leukaemia treatment while I breast-fed Matthew. My sympathy for the medical team is immense, all were patient with my view that I had to give Matthew the very best start in life. At the time I didn't think I was taking a stupid risk with myself, just balancing the needs of my baby with a small delay.

But after giving birth, my high white cell count was making everybody nervous, and Professor Goldman arranged for my blood to be filtered at the Hammersmith.

On the way to London Adrian surprised me by saying, 'So, are we going to ask Goldman about having another baby?'

I stared at him with eyes open wide.

'Do you mean it Ade?'

'I heard you the other day Fran, and I'll back you all the way, but don't hold your breath for him to say yes.'

'You do want this as much as I do?'

'We've always planned to have two children, and I'm a hundred per cent committed to that, but I want you to realise we're worried about your blood count and must do the best thing for your leukaemia. We should be guided by Professor Goldman on this. If he says no, we have a beautiful perfect son already.'

'Yes, and I'll always be thankful for that, but we planned for two.'

'I was an only child and it was still a proper family. It wouldn't be the end of the world.'

'But it won't do any harm asking.'

'I agree, but don't expect Goldman to be thrilled by the idea.'

At the consultation Matthew kicked the air with chubby little legs, oblivious of the miracle of his existence, or any inkling that the studious professor was largely responsible for it.

Professor Goldman leaned over the carrytot and peered over his half moon glasses, 'So this is Matthew who caused all the fuss is it?'

When we discussed the issue of breast-feeding, he gave me a maximum period of three months without treatment while I fed Matthew.

At the end of the appointment he put his pen down and said, 'Well I think that's everything, you can go through to the ward now for filtration.'

I leaned forward, 'There is one more thing I want to ask you Professor Goldman,' I said, swallowing nervously and looking down at the floor. 'I want us to have another baby.'

There was a moment of absolute stillness in the room. Then Professor Goldman's phone rang. He picked it up and spoke briefly. I didn't hear a single word he said, but I kept staring at the marks on the old lino and thinking, 'please, please say yes.'

Professor Goldman put down the receiver and put his head in his hands. He rubbed his eyes and then started to chuckle. 'Oh Fran, you're amazing. You're playing with fire, and you know all the risks, we've been over them before. If you're absolutely dead set on having another go, you'd better be quick. But I would prefer us to store some fertilised embryos so you can have a child after transplant.'

'I'd rather give it a try now and if that fails, then consider storing an embryo later. I want to try to have another child naturally.'

'Fair enough, you've recovered from the birth, but I cannot sanction any attempt at conception until we get your cell count down through leucapheresis. Once your cell count is down to reasonable levels, then I'll give you three months to conceive, just like before, and if nothing happens by then, you have no choice but to abandon conception and go for a transplant. Your time is running out Fran.'

'I know Professor Goldman, I know, but this means everything to me.'

'And Adrian, what about you? What do you want?'

Adrian leaned forward and looked directly at Professor Goldman. 'More than anything, I want us to have the family we planned, but I'm putting more emphasis on Fran's health than she is, because I want to be certain she's well enough before we go ahead. The timing needs to be as good as possible, but I'm one hundred per cent committed to having another child. What's your professional opinion?'

'In a way the situation this time is more difficult. Before you conceived Matthew you had been on *Interferon* so your leukaemia was under control, and the positive effects of *Interferon* would have lasted into the pregnancy. This time you won't have a kick-start. As soon as you finish breast-feeding, I'll have to put you on *Hydoroxyurea* to kill off the white cells, but it isn't a cure, and it won't do anything at all to help the cause of your problem. I'm afraid a second pregnancy in your condition carries greater risks than the first. But if you know that and decide to take the risk, I'll try and help.' He smiled again, 'You're a rare one Fran.'

Nowadays, when I recall these critical moments of decision that hung on the support of Professor Goldman and the medical team, I shudder with the seriousness of my demands. At the time I was blinkered by an overwhelming desire to have a family, which was a greater force even than my need to survive. I was utterly single-minded.

But now the issues seem very complex, and in retrospect I know I asked my doctors for one miracle after another. In hindsight, putting myself in Professor Goldman's shoes, I'm amazed by the support, generosity and understanding he showed us. I surely pushed the experts to the limits of their tolerance, but I hope that in doing so, I helped others who come after me to have choice.

We went out of the consulting room to show off Matthew to the excited team of nurses and staff. Everybody crowded round the carrytot car-seat to coo over and admire the miracle baby they'd seen in the newspapers.

Before the filtration of my blood, I breast-fed Matthew and hoped he wouldn't get hungry in the few hours while I was plugged into the machine. I wasn't worried about the treatment at all, only scared that Matthew would need me, as he hadn't ever been bottle-fed.

The filtration wasn't painful but frustrating. A tube was inserted into my arm and the blood flowed out of my vein into a filtration unit which sections off the white cells and platelets into a bag. The blood is then returned into a vein in the other arm. All I felt was the needle at insertion but I had to lie very still during the process. Now and again a nurse gave me a drink of milk through a straw.

It felt good to know that my blood was clean and healthy again, and Adrian said Matthew hadn't cried once, he was absolutely fine.

By the time Matthew was three months old, life had begun to settle into a pattern of normality. Apart from frequent visits to Warwick Hospital and the Hammersmith, I could pretend I was just like any other new mother. And it felt so good.

But that autumn came an event totally outside normal experience. Anthony Nolan invited Adrian and me to their annual function, a champagne reception held in a very smart London barracks. Each year the guest list consists of a few donors and patients, people who have raised a lot of money for the cause, and celebrities who have supported the charity. It's a thank-you and a chance to bring like-minded supporters together.

Ever since childhood, I had been an ardent royalist, and I was thrilled to hear the Duchess of Kent would be at the event, in her role as patron of Anthony Nolan. I was truly excited to be invited, and went shopping with my Mum to find a suitable outfit.

'Fancy a Bevan meeting royalty!' Mum grinned, 'you'd better not let the side down.' Although she said this, it never occurred to me I would meet the Duchess, I wasn't even hopeful of picking her out in the crowd.

The big day came, I went to the hairdresser and had my hair put up into a French pleat, and when Adrian and I arrived at the venue, I was stunned into silence, my excitement turning into nervousness. Inside the entrance hall we saw an imposing flight of stairs lined with uniformed men holding impossibly shiny trumpets. I had never been anywhere like it in my life, and I was overawed.

We made it up the staircase somehow, and were ushered into a beautiful panelled hall filled with smiling dignitaries and smart guests. The room hummed with chamber music and the social chatter of the well-to-do. Adrian and I knew nobody at all, and stood clutching our glasses of champagne while trying to blend into the background.

I whispered to Adrian, 'Oh no, who on earth are we going to talk to?'

But although we knew nobody, people seemed to recognise us. One or two staff from Anthony Nolan introduced themselves because they had heard of our fund-raising with IBM and everybody was full of thanks for our efforts. Whenever I had the chance, I sneaked a look across the room at the Duchess of Kent. I recognised her from the Wimbledon coverage, but she looked more lovely and serene in real life.

Then I began talking to a girl called Ellen who had been diagnosed with leukaemia at the same time as me and was also looking for a donor. I started to relax as I chatted to her and her husband, and began enjoying myself.

Suddenly there was a tap on my shoulder and I turned to look round. Standing beside me was Tony Morland, the Chief Executive of Anthony Nolan who I recognised from a previous meeting, and right beside him was the Duchess of Kent.

'Excuse me Fran, I would like to introduce you to the Duchess. She has been most interested to hear about your little boy, Matthew.'

Immediately my heart leaped into my mouth and I knew my neck and cheeks would be reddening into the annoying blotches that started whenever I was nervous. I shook their outstretched hands and couldn't think of anything to say except a small 'Hello.'

But within moments, the Duchess put me at ease. Her interest in me and my desperate desire to have children was evident at once. I addressed her as 'Your Royal Highness' and she corrected me with a smile,

'Please don't call me that, just call me Katherine.'

Our conversation seemed to last for a long time, but was probably only minutes, and my overriding memory of that meeting was her genuine heart-felt love. She was wonderful to me, and thoroughly excited to hear all about baby Matthew. She shared in our joy and made me promise to keep in touch, and let her know my progress in the search for a donor.

'But I don't know your address!' I stammered, and she laughed warmly, telling me to write to her at the Palace where the letter would reach her. She asked for my address to send something to Matthew, but I had no pen or paper in my bag. So she made me promise to write, and as she walked away, I remember thinking how hard it must be to be royal and famous, because nobody behaves normally around you. I certainly hadn't, and kept asking Adrian, 'Did I make a complete fool of myself? Was I an idiot?'

A few moments later Adrian scribbled our address down on a piece of paper.

'You can't give it to her, we can't just pass her our address!' I yelped.

'She asked for it Fran, and I can recognise sincerity when I see it. That woman is completely sincere.' And so he walked over to the Duchess and gave her our address.

I never dreamed we would hear any more about it, but I treasured the memory of our meeting.

November blew itself into a chilly December and I began socialising with other young mums in our village. It was very important to me that I behaved and appeared just like any normal new mother. Adrian and I had attended NCT childbirth classes before Matthew was born, and I'd become very close to a girl in the group called Dee. She gave birth to baby Jade a week before I had Matthew, and we became closer than ever once the children were born. Dee stood out from all the other girls I met at this time, because she always treated me as a normal person. Since we first met, she has been interested in me first, and my illness last. Dee never asked how I was, or pried, although she let me cry on her shoulder if and when I wanted. Matthew's birth was in the middle of the heaviest media coverage, when I yearned for normality more than ever. Dee made me feel ordinary, accepted, just a new Mum with normal concerns. That's why we became, and remain, especially close to this day.

One frosty morning before Christmas, I invited Dee and another girl from NCT for coffee. We were enjoying a chat and the chance to swap baby stories, when my front doorbell rang. I opened the door and was shocked to see a man holding a box from Harrods.

'No sorry, it's not for me,' I said to the delivery driver.

'Are you Mrs Burke?'

'Yes,'

'Well it's for you then, can you sign here please?'

'But there's no way I've ordered anything from Harrods.'

'Then it's a present – you lucky girl!' he said grinning.

I set the box on the floor until the mums and babies had gone home, and as soon as they left I rang Adrian. Since my diagnosis, that had become my immediate first response, it never occurred to me to open the parcel.

When I got through I asked 'Have you ordered anything from Harrods because we've just had a parcel delivered?'

'No sweetheart, it's nothing to do with me.'

'It's a complete mystery – who do we know who shops at Harrods?' I asked.

Suddenly Adrian's voice changed, 'Maybe it's a bomb Fran. I want you to take the box outside and leave it at the bottom of the garden. Don't touch it until I come home.'

Very carefully I carried the mystery parcel to the furthest corner of the garden and left it there until it started to rain when I brought it in gingerly. Looking back it seems ludicrous that we overreacted so much – I remember my brother saying, 'Who on earth would be sending you a bomb Fran? For heaven's sake!'

Adrian phoned me back and said, 'I've been thinking about that parcel and it may be from the Duchess of Kent. She promised to send Matthew something, so you'd better open it.'

Very carefully, while Adrian was waiting on the line, I opened the box. Inside I found a Lullaby light show for Matthew and a little card wishing him 'Happy Christmas, with love from Katherine'. I was absolutely gob-smacked and delighted, and broke all my usual rules about waiting for presents until the 25th by giving it to Matthew straight away.

That afternoon, as the winter sun set and his nursery became dark, we played with the light show, and he laughed at the pretty patterns thrown onto his ceiling while the music tinkled.

'You lucky, lucky boy,' I told him, 'that's from the Duchess of Kent and she's in the royal family!' and he only gurgled and smiled.

I wrote and thanked the Duchess at once and never thought our paths would cross again.

The Anthony Nolan champagne reception in November marked the end of my period of grace for breast-feeding, and Professor Goldman put me back on *Hydoroxyurea* to control my white cell count. He asked me to take the drug until January and then took me off for a couple of weeks to clear my system of its side effects. Then he gave me the go-ahead I had prayed so hard for, to allow us to try for our precious second child.

Adrian suggested that after the success of our holiday in Antigua, we should book another special holiday to try and conceive. So we took a last minute package to Barbados in February and Matthew had his very first flight. Not a bad first destination at six months old!

Throughout the holiday I hoped I may be pregnant, and we had the happiest time of our lives. It was our first visit to Barbados, and our first holiday with Matthew, a double miracle because we didn't think we would have a child, never mind be planning another. Matthew was the only baby in the hotel and everyone made an enormous fuss of him, and he rose to the occasion with style. We were unashamedly proud parents and felt just like a normal family.

On the last night, we sat chatting with a couple who had become holiday friends and I told Christine how sad I felt to be leaving Barbados. Then I confided I was afraid of returning home and finding I wasn't pregnant, because I knew the end of the line was near.

Christine turned to me, 'You never know, you could be pregnant now. I believe you are so just wait and see.'

Her words meant so much, and gave me a little ray of hope that she may be right, I could be carrying another child just like Matthew.

There were two exceptional moments in the holiday, first a chance meeting with Luciano Pavarotti – the famous opera singer – who was staying on the island. He chatted with us and we took photographs for Adrian's Mum who thinks the world of Pavarotti.

Our wedding day, 1989

Days at IBM

ii

(Above)
My husband,
Adrian

(Right)
Adrian,
my brother Nick,
and I

Off on the bike ride with Terry Butcher and Adrian

Matthew, my gift from God

Meeting the Duchess of Kent (above, with my parents)

Our car in the European Express Rally

The family complete

Adrian with
Sebastian

Matthew and I

Sebastian

My boys whom I had to leave behind

At last, receiving the marrow

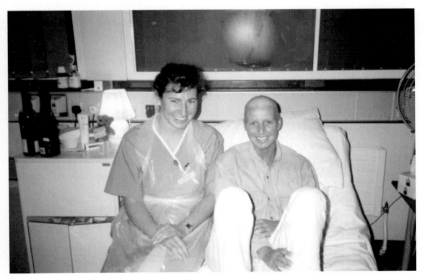

The only photo on record of my bald head,
with my named nurse, Kath

Three very important men in my life. Professor John
Goldman, Adrian and the Transplant Manager, Simon Rule

(Above) Saying goodbye to Professor Goldman

(Below) My brother Nick, as a donor

Dee and I in a
moment of madness

The ring in the trailer

My donor, Anne

Three good reasons to survive

Happy Days

The second was a meeting on the beach where we started a conversation with a friendly American couple. They made a lot of fuss of Matthew, and after a while I confided, 'He's very special to us because I've got leukaemia and we didn't think he would ever be born. He's a miracle.'

Immediately both the man and wife fell silent and she looked pale despite her golden tan.

I thought, 'oh no, what on earth have I said?'

Eventually the woman spoke in a soft American drawl, 'That's very weird because our own son died of leukaemia when he was sixteen.'

'I'm so sorry, I didn't mean to upset you.' I said, wishing I had never mentioned my illness.

'That's OK. Ever since he died, we've worked for the cause in New York where we have set up a special leukaemia hospital, and we've invested in research labs to try and find out what causes leukaemia in the first place. We come here on holiday once a year as our rest, we have money you see, but we don't have our son.'

We talked together for a long time, sharing our story with this family who had suffered such terrible loss and pain because of leukaemia. Eight years later we're still in touch.

Our meeting made me even more thankful to have Matthew, but more terrified that my own time was running out.

Chapter Eight

Sebastian

ೞ ೞ ೞ ೞ

As soon as we returned home from Barbados I bought a pregnancy kit and it was positive. Christine was right, and I was over the moon. Immediately Adrian and I planned to ask Christine and Tom to be godparents to our second child.

Unbelievably, I had conceived Matthew in the first month, and this time during the second. I'm eternally grateful for the amazing blessing of early conception, and in hindsight it seems even more of a miracle than it did then. I'll never know why the leukaemia and the pressure of having only three months to conceive didn't stop my body from cooperating.

Once the official news broke a few months later, we had more media coverage, especially poignant now baby Matthew could be included in the photographs. Most of the coverage at this time was negative and critical, suggesting we were wrong to bring children into the world when their mother was unlikely to live.

The press reports made me very, very angry, I hated seeing us painted as an irresponsible couple who gave no thought to consequences. Also at this time, I noticed criticism from some medical staff, one or two of whom hinted we were making wrong choices. Their attitude didn't make me angry, because they were having to treat me and pick up the pieces of my illness, but I want this book to set the record straight and explain that Adrian and I could not have given the subject more serious thought.

We had discussed the pros and cons, the risks and joys of having a family, and we made our decisions based on our own unique circumstances. Without total agreement from each other, neither of us would have pursued this course, and I mean this most sincerely, even I would have abandoned my hopes if Adrian couldn't take the burden of raising children alone. I had to live with the leukaemia, and Adrian faced living without a wife. We knew the seriousness of our choices.

I had always planned to return to work at IBM part-time after Matthew's birth, but although my career was important, leukaemia had changed my outlook on life for ever. My friend Dee was a child-minder and had agreed to mind Matthew for me, which was a perfect arrangement as he adored her daughter.

As the time to return to IBM drew nearer, I became increasingly worried about leaving Matthew when my future was so uncertain. A week before my start date, my boss visited to confirm my role and plan my retraining. As we sat together in the study I said, 'I'm so worried about doing this, I don't know how much time I have left, or if working is the right thing to do. Maybe I shouldn't come back?'

He was very understanding and supportive. 'Why don't you come back and try it, and just see what happens. Only you can make the decision Fran, you've always said you would come back to IBM, but you can change your mind at any time.'

So a week later I dusted off one of my work suits and took Matthew to Dee's house. When she opened her door Dee screeched, 'Come in quick before the neighbours see you – I've never seen you out of leggings and a baggy jumper!'

But it didn't work out. As I sat at my new desk, in the familiar surroundings of the open plan office in Warwick, I realised that every single day with Matthew was too precious and valuable. Thoughts raced through my mind … I don't know how long I've got left … I can't be away from Matthew because every single day is special.

Being at work felt wrong, and guilt overwhelmed me. I knew I had risked everything to have Matthew, so it certainly should be me who was bringing him up. So I talked to Adrian and went to see my new manager. When I walked into his office and said, 'I'm so sorry – I just can't do this,' he amazed me with his understanding and concern. My resignation was accepted and I went home with joy in my heart.

There were many things about IBM I missed, especially the people and their wonderful support, but my overwhelming commitment was to my husband and child, and I think all my colleagues understood that. My gratitude to IBM will never fade, it was more than a job, and the company proved to be much more than just an employer.

Late into my second pregnancy was the last and perhaps finest charity campaign. Dave Kelly, my good and loyal friend, offered us the chance to raise money and awareness for leukaemia by taking part in the 1993 London to Milan European Express Rally. This is a race by sponsored sports cars from London Victoria attempting to beat the *Orient Express* into Milan. Dave's Mitsubishi garage donated a 3000GT car and persuaded Pentti Arikkala to race it, with Adrian as co-driver. Pentti had won the RAC Lombard rally a few years earlier, and it was a chance in a lifetime for Adrian who was given permission to drive me to Victoria for the race start in the passion-red sports car.

The *Leamington Courier* ran a high profile campaign to support us, and a reader's competition with a first prize of two tickets on the *Orient Express* for the actual race. A lovely young couple won the tickets, but nearly didn't make it on board when they mislaid a passport!

The Anthony Nolan Bone Marrow Trust gave us a big send-off with Linda Robson, Fiona Fullerton and Stirling

Moss at Victoria station, then the boys accelerated away with the pack of revving sports cars, and the Orient Express pulled out with our prize-winners waving madly out of the window. The excitement turned to quiet anti-climax for me left with spectators at the station – we would hear no more until the race was over. I had no way of contacting Ade or finding out where he was, knowing only that they had planned a road route through France and Italy, and he was navigating. I only hoped Pentti had enough patience!

A couple of days later, Mitsubishi generously flew me out to Milan for the finish, and still we had no idea where the boys were. But just as I arrived to check in at the hotel reception, I was amazed to see Pentti rush in.

I leapt towards him, 'What are you doing here? Is everything OK?' I asked breathlessly.

'Yes, fine.'

'Where's Ade?'

'Parking the car,' he said, and I burst out laughing as he grabbed my arm, 'We've won Fran!'

It was true. Our car, sponsored by the *Leamington Courier* who had been so supportive of me, had come in first. We were presented with a trophy at the finale held in a castle outside Milan, and it seemed like a fairy-tale. It was something else I would delight in telling my children as they grew up. As we watched the fireworks and celebrated in style, I vowed to do everything to make sure I would be there to tell them myself.

I returned to the routine of motherhood and one afternoon came home with the weekly food shopping, unlocked the front door and clicked the play button on our answer machine, just like any other day. I was settling Matthew as the machine played aloud, 'Hello Fran, this is Fritz from the Hammersmith. We think we've found a bone marrow donor match for you, and we should arrange a transplant as soon as possible after the birth. Please call me back.'

Immediately I dropped the bag of shopping and sank down at the bottom of the stairs. This was the most frightening piece of news I had ever heard in my life. Much, much more frightening than the initial diagnosis. That had been a heart-breaking shock, but this was pure terror.

I knew the consultant whom we called Fritz, and liked and trusted him. I replayed his answer phone message over and over, and asked myself why I was feeling so utterly frozen with fear. My whole body was shaking, and a thousand thoughts rushed through my mind. Ever since my leukaemia diagnosis I had anticipated this moment, certain I would be ecstatic to hear the wonderful news. I had expected to be overjoyed at receiving a glimmer of hope and a chance of life.

But the reality was nothing like that. Ahead of me was the awful truth that I was going ahead with the biggest medical gamble of all, to risk my life for a kill or cure transplant. I was desperate to live, but a transplant would take me to the point of death, and could actually kill me.

Now there was no longer any excuse. It had been such a comfort to be able to say to people, 'Oh yes I need to have a transplant, we're waiting for one, but I don't have a donor yet.' Being in limbo had felt very safe, and I had convinced my husband, my family and myself that I was fully committed to a transplant, if only they could find a donor.

But now, on the foot of the stairs I admitted the heart-aching truth to myself. I had never wanted a transplant, I didn't want one now, and I was chilled to the bone with the fear of it.

I had always known that any time in the next couple of years, my condition may deteriorate and become acute, and that would be the end, but somehow the danger seemed vague and distant. Apart from my time on *Interferon*, I had felt so well I could often forget I even had leukaemia, only hospital appointments confirmed it was still present.

And suddenly with one phone message, the limbo had ended. Against all the odds, despite my very rare antigens, a donor had been found, so my choice had been made for me. I knew I had to go through with this, my only chance of a cure, and understood the scale of risk involved – I had a beautiful son and a baby on the way – and now I may lose my life by trying to save it.

I longed to turn the clock back and be safe again, the adrenaline made me want to run away with Matthew and Adrian to hide somewhere quiet, dark and safe where the terrible word 'transplant' would never be mentioned again.

My shaking got worse, and the fear rose within me. Matthew was blissfully asleep in his baby seat, and eventually I plucked up the courage to ring Adrian. It should have been told as good news, but after the months of praying for this, it felt like disaster.

Fifteen minutes later, I was still sitting by the phone at the foot of the stairs, and suddenly a new thought struck me, 'who on earth is it?' A burning desire was triggered to know which selfless and incredible person could offer to do this for me. I knew the process of giving bone marrow isn't particularly pleasant, and I was staggered that someone had volunteered to put themselves through it for my sake. Again this was a complete reversal from the previous two years when I had wondered why everyone in the world didn't volunteer to be a bone marrow donor.

Now I thought, 'I pray to God that one day I manage to meet this person and thank them for offering to do this fabulous thing for me.'

I did get off the stairs eventually, and ate and played with Matthew, but I remained lost in thought and fear for many days.

The Hammersmith arranged an appointment for us to discuss the potential transplant and we attended with trepidation. Adrian was much more positive than me, certain this was the best news in the world for us, positive as always that we would get through. His optimism helped to buoy me up.

Professor Goldman confirmed that a good match had indeed been found, but all he would tell us was the donor was female, married with two children and living in the UK. All my most persuasive lines of questioning revealed nothing else, and I gleaned no more for the next three years.

Anthony Nolan has the entirely sensible regulation that no patient ever knows their donor, and identity is never revealed before a transplant. The emotional complexity of a transplant is such that any contact or communication would be too unsettling, and if the operation failed, the potential grief for the donor would be unbearable. I knew and accepted all these things, but an immense inquisitiveness about my donor remained.

The initial tests had revealed a six-antigen match, and Professor Goldman thought my chance of a successful transplant looked good. He believed that in my somewhat difficult and unusual case, we would be unlikely to improve on this level of match.

As usual at every single consultation, Adrian was taking notes and going into a deep level of detail with Professor Goldman while he explained the basis of accepting a donor.

'There isn't an absolute direct relationship between a good antigen match and a successful bone marrow transplant. There are many factors we don't understand. Some patients go into a transplant with a poor match and have a very successful outcome, others have a great match but don't pull through. It isn't a precise science, we have to weigh up all the risks and try to lower them.'

'What do you think of Fran's chances with this donor? Is it a good match?'

'I think it's not good, but it's not bad.'

I was really struggling with this vagueness, 'Excuse me Professor Goldman but you've lost me here,' I said, 'surely you can tell whether it's good or bad. You've seen hundreds of cases.'

He looked at me with the blank stare we had come to know so well, 'We never stop weighing up all the factors

Fran, and every transplant teaches us something, but I have to be honest with you and say there is no simple logical formula of answering your question. I wish there were. But in my opinion, this is a good enough match for a transplant. With your antigens you were very lucky to find someone as close as this.'

I began to realise that I was very fortunate to have found a donor at all, and Professor Goldman's faith was infectious. But Adrian and I decided not to tell anyone about the potential transplant until after our baby was born. We wanted to come to terms with the concept ourselves, and we needed to focus all our energy on the pregnancy and birth. I have to admit our other reservation about the news getting out, was our fear of a media field day on 'Fran finds a donor – but refuses transplant'. Any irresponsible coverage during late pregnancy would have been hard to take.

But once the news began to sink in, I experienced many of the emotions I'd always imagined I should feel when I found a donor; relief, thankfulness and hope.

There were a few special people whom I could trust with the news. Our parents of course, who were nervous but absolutely supportive, showing an almost tangible relief, now they could dare to hope for my future.

And my other confidante was the Duchess of Kent. We had begun corresponding after my first letter thanking her for the lullaby light show, and I was amazed and honoured by her evident desire to stay in touch, as I had never expected to hear from her again. But Tony Morland of Anthony Nolan often told me the Duchess had asked for news of my progress.

So now I wrote and let her know that Anthony Nolan had found a donor for me. I have always suffered from low confidence and poor self esteem, and kept asking myself, 'why would such a famous and beautiful person be interested in me?' But there was no denying that she was.

A short time later the Duchess sent the first of several beautiful cards, signing as Katherine, the card covered with flowers and verses, and I knew she had begun a time of prayer for me which came to prove life-sustaining in the months ahead.

Matthew's first birthday was a quiet one. We had a small family party tea that was more for the parents' benefit than Matthew and his best friend Jade, who were oblivious as we helped eat their chocolate train cake. As I photographed my son, looking so cute in his high chair exactly a year after his miracle birth, I wondered if I would live to see his next party.

This pregnancy was more difficult. My white cell count escalated quickly this time, and just as Professor Goldman had predicted, I missed the benefit of the kick start given by *Interferon* first time round. I had been without treatment for a full twelve months to have Matthew, then after a short bout on *Hydroxyurea*, I had lived a further six months without drugs. There were still another five months to reach full-term.

Professor Goldman decided my blood must be filtered to remove the excessive white cells and arranged sessions for me at the Haematology ward in Warwick Hospital, so saving me the tiring trip to London. I was very thankful as I was becoming too weak to travel.

But after the first filtration by leucapheresis, my white cell count bounced back again very quickly and I became pretty scared. The trips to Warwick hospital became more and more frequent during the last three months of pregnancy, and I knew time was against me. Despite fortnightly then weekly filtrations, my cell count returned to levels high enough to cause haemorrhage during child-birth.

I had always hoped to have a son and a daughter, to mirror the family I had grown up in, and don't deny that I carried a secret hope our second child would be a girl. At the last scan of pregnancy, I hoped the sex might be detectable and asked the young radiologist, 'I'd love to know the sex of the baby, is it at all obvious?' I knew hospital policy was to withhold such information, and didn't expect an answer.

I could tell by her grin that the radiologist had been asked the question before. As she moved the ultra-sound beam across my stomach she said, 'Yes, it's pretty obvious to me.'

Although she didn't actually say it, I knew what she meant, our second child was a boy too. But I felt no disappointment, and instead began longing to see the face of our new son.

I made it to eight and a half months, and although I had enjoyed both pregnancies, this time I was more worried. The effects of my leukaemia were getting worse, and my body was protesting too much.

But stubborn as ever, I tried to persuade Mr Hughes to let me have a natural birth. 'Please can we just try to let the baby be born naturally?'

I could tell from his dear, sympathetic face, that I had asked one question too far. 'No Fran, it would be stupid and irresponsible of me to allow it. Your white cell count is too high this time and we need to intervene.'

'OK,' I said, 'I know it can't be safe if you don't agree.'

'So I'm going to book you in for a planned caesarean at thirty-eight weeks.'

'But that's two weeks early, what about the baby?'

'The baby will be absolutely fine, and it's much better for you. Remember, there's the issue of taking cells from the umbilical cord too, so Dr Rose needs to be standing by, and it will be safer and easier to have the whole thing planned. Even though you have a potential donor, we want to take the baby's cells in case we need them for you in future.'

'Would it be different if I'd managed to have Matthew without a caesarean? I really wanted to do it properly this time.'

'Fran, you've achieved miracles with these pregnancies, please let us help you finish it safely.'

I agreed of course, but with a twinge of sadness that I would never have a normal birth. But then nothing about my case was truly normal, and my overriding desire was to ensure the baby's safe arrival into the world.

So on the morning of 28th October 1993, we took Matthew to stay with my parents and Adrian drove me to the Warneford Hospital in Leamington Spa. We arrived at lunch time and on the way to theatre I bumped into Mr Hughes, my gynaecologist, who was wearing an operating gown and wellingtons! I was absolutely terrified when I saw the boots and said 'What on earth are you going to do to me?' I had visions of a floor awash with body fluids, and it didn't help my nerves.

This time was very different from the operation with Matthew. Then I had been worn out after hours of labour, and when they anaesthetised me I honestly hadn't cared what they did. But now I was wide awake and aware of what was going on. As I slipped away into unconsciousness I remember thinking, 'here we go again, I hope I come out of this.'

Adrian waited outside theatre and said it seemed to take an age, I think the harvesting of umbilical cord cells took a while to perform. But the caesarean went well and I woke up in the recovery room with Adrian standing over me, his face flushed with relief as I opened my eyes.

'It's another boy!' he said, delighted, and evidently relieved. The staff lifted our new son onto my chest and I felt a wave of profound love and delight pour over me and seep through my body. I dozed in and out of consciousness hearing a clatter of metal implements and Adrian asking 'Are you OK Fran? We've got a boy, he's beautiful!' and I was only aware of the feeling of a tiny life next to my heart. I wanted everybody to leave me alone, so I could sleep on, secure in the knowledge that our precious son was in the world, and safe.

The baby weighed in at 6lb 14oz and he was as beautiful as his big brother. This time we didn't have a name ready because we hadn't been able to find another name meaning gift from God. Before the birth we had short-listed Sebastian and Peter, and as I drifted in and out of consciousness I remember saying to Adrian, 'Does he look like a Sebastian or a Peter?' I was aware of the nurse calling to Adrian, 'Does the baby have a name yet? What shall I write on the wrist-band?'

Adrian replied 'I'm not sure yet' and the nurse tagged him 'Baby Burke' for a few days, until we knew him well enough to decide he had to be Sebastian.

The baby's first visitor was the receptionist from maternity out-patients who I knew well from many check-ups. She had just finished her shift, and I remember her saying 'I don't think Fran knows I'm here,' but I was aware that she, Adrian, and most importantly, the new baby, were beside me.

The sensation of our new-born child lying on me was one of the greatest feelings of my life, and it was particularly special this time to know the baby was safe after such a worrying pregnancy.

I didn't wake fully until I was back on the ward and heard Adrian saying, 'Fran, none of the theatre staff could get over the size of the baby's feet – he's got enormous feet!' I lay and looked at our child and was amazed to find a new supply of love for him which was separate and additional to my love for Matthew. It sounds silly now, but before he was born I feared we could never love another child in the same way as the first, but I couldn't have been more wrong. I guess it's the same for all parents, every time a child is born, it brings a new, immense capacity for love in you with it.

I desperately wanted Matthew to see his new brother, but things didn't go smoothly, and the baby's entry into the world was heralded with chaos.

The Warneford Hospital, maternity unit and all, was scheduled for permanent closure the day after my caesarean, and an ambulance had been booked to move us to Warwick Hospital. But that day, when Sebastian was only twenty-four hours old, I had a major haemorrhage. Staff were having a party to celebrate the closure of the hospital and I lay in my room, bleeding badly, feeling faint, and knowing something was going wrong. I had been told not to call a nurse except in genuine emergency. Eventually I rang the bell and lay listening to the sound of laughter and celebration down the corridor.

When a nurse responded, the look on her face told me I needed help. Mr Hughes reacted immediately and contacted Professor Goldman on his home number and took advice on how to help me.

The bleeding was horrendous and profuse, and my body just couldn't heal from surgery. My problem was a lack of platelets caused by the huge numbers of mutant white cells in my blood. Professor Goldman told Mr Hughes to give me a platelet transfusion and the Warneford responded very quickly. I felt extremely wary about receiving someone else's blood, it was the first time I had needed a blood product from a stranger, and I feared all sorts of complications. Until then I'd been lucky enough to manage with my own blood, taken in advance and returned to me when needed.

But baby Sebastian was by my side and I felt so positive that Adrian would have been proud of me, 'I'm coming home, and what's got to be done has got to be done. It will be worth it to have my boys.'

The very next day my situation had stabilised and I was allowed to have the visitor I longed for. My parents brought Matthew in and it was a perfect moment. At last my family was complete and I couldn't stop smiling as I watched baby Matthew staring into the cot. After two terrible years I had the children I had always prayed for, and experienced a sensation of total peace and bliss. I wanted to forget the leukaemia and have a little while enjoying my new family.

Chapter Nine

A Bomb in the Attic

ᘛ ᘚ ᘛ ᘚ

Having two boys was hard work but my life was truly idyllic. When I look back to the first year with the babies, it was probably the happiest time of my life. I had my hands full, but at last I had everything I'd ever wanted, two healthy children and a wonderful marriage. I had no regrets about leaving work, and enjoyed every day.

Sebastian's first Christmas came and went. In the early spring we did simple, ordinary things together, messy painting at home on cold wet days, and trips to the park to feed the ducks when the sun shone.

But unlike all the other mums I knew, I had an increasing pressure looming on my horizon, the pressure from not just one medic, but tens of them, telling me it was time for my transplant.

From the day Sebastian was born, the Hammersmith was ready to go ahead with the transplant and we had many, many debates about the timing. There were one or two fixed and definite facts already. My parents would care for the boys while I was in isolation after transplant, and Adrian would move in with me at the Hammersmith throughout isolation. Without these key supporters in place, I could never have gone ahead with the treatment.

I was afraid the medics would lose all sympathy with my case if I delayed now I had two boys and a donor in place.

But I knew how much the babies needed me, and hid myself away, afraid to face the inevitable decision.

Adrian and I skirted the issue until one day we had a real heart to heart. It was time to face up to the future, because whichever way you looked at it, my time was running out.

We opened Adrian's fat and well-thumbed notebook, now two years old, and reviewed the opinion of the professionals. Logical and methodical as ever, Adrian plotted a vertical line to indicate where we all stood on the scale of preference for timing of a transplant.

Fritz, my transplant manager at the Hammersmith, was more anxious than anyone. He had insinuated a second pregnancy was madness, and he reminded me frequently that I was playing with fire. As far as he was concerned, tomorrow wasn't soon enough for my transplant. So we plotted him on the very top of the scale.

'What about Goldman?' asked Adrian.

'He's relaxed about it,' I replied, 'and he's never put pressure on us.'

So Adrian plotted him about half way up the scale. He drew my Dad nearer the top under Fritz, and my Mum somewhere in the middle.'

'What about you Ade?' I asked.

'I'm guided by Goldman, so I don't think we're running a high risk. For me, the practical considerations are vital. We need time to plan care for the boys, because we'll be away from them for several months, and we want to think about the best time of year. It would be far better for you to recover from a transplant in the summer than the winter.'

'But it's spring already. I don't want it to be so soon.'

'What about next spring then?'

'In another year's time?'

'Yes. By then Sebastian would be eighteen months old and you will have had a good long time with both of them.'

'That would be fantastic, I could cope with that.'

'So how do you feel about the risk Fran? I'm plotting myself near the bottom, is it essential to rush it, what do you think?'

I looked out at our garden and acknowledged what was in my heart. But I didn't say it. 'Same as you, put me next to you,' I said.

But deep down, if I'm really honest, eighteen months was still too soon for me. I wanted my time with the children to go on for ever, undisturbed and unspoilt. A delay suited me because I was more terrified of a transplant than any horror life could throw at me. I didn't want to leave the boys, and was afraid I wouldn't survive. At the core of me was a sick and twisted contradiction, knowing I was playing with fire by delaying life-saving treatment, but unable to hurry into it.

Like the termination of pregnancy two years before, I was facing a truly impossible choice; I could refuse a transplant, go on living with the boys, and then I would certainly die. Or I could choose a transplant for their sake, and take a 45% chance on coming through. It was as bad as a game of Russian roulette that I had never asked to play.

We added the other medics to Adrian's graph and the only one who stood near the top was Fritz the transplant manager. But as he was nearing the end of his year in post, we knew he would disappear from the equation. On balance the decision was easy, we decided that at our next consultation we would ask Professor Goldman to delay my transplant for a year until May 1995.

When we arrived for our appointment the procedure was exactly the same as every other week. We checked in at out-patients and had a visit from Professor Goldman's secretary Karen Linfield, who was always wonderful to us. We knew her well, because while many leukaemia patients have a transplant soon after diagnosis, we had been around for ages, like a couple of bad apples! She had even fielded media approaches for us, and if we took the boys to hospital, she watched them while we had our appointment. Just as he had with Linda Hartwell at Anthony Nolan, Adrian struck up a rapport with Karen.

Then, every week, we called at the hospital shop where Adrian bought a newspaper, a couple of magazines and several large bars of chocolate. We took them to the drab waiting room and began the weekly wait of at least two hours, until our turn came to see Professor Goldman.

This is the absolute truth, as we sat waiting, Adrian worked his way through his paper, magazines and chocolate. Even though he did it every single week, I never ceased to be stunned. I could only manage to sit and look with horror and fascination at the other patients, who were in various stages of treatment. Some had terrible skin problems brought on by Graft versus Host, some were shaking, some bald. But Adrian was oblivious to it all, he munched and read, read and munched, lost in his own little world.

I'm embarrassed to admit this next bit, but early in the relationship with Professor Goldman, Adrian had set himself a challenge to lighten up the heavy atmosphere of the discussions. Although he was utterly serious about my case, Adrian decided to try and make Professor Goldman laugh or at least smile at every single consultation. The challenge began because the professor is a very quiet and private man. He always kept patients at arm's length, and didn't ever divulge personal information. As such, he was completely professional.

After the first few appointments, Adrian commented to me that he had never seen Professor Goldman smile, and decided to do something about it. So every week, from then until now, (and I assume the poor man had no idea), Adrian tried to raise a laugh. And when Professor Goldman smiles, we all laugh, and I have a secret hope that we have a special relationship.

To my utter relief on this occasion, Professor Goldman agreed that with close monitoring of my blood and no further complications, he would delay my transplant until the following May. I was absolutely relieved and delighted, and prayed the year would be the slowest of my life.

All our parents were overjoyed I had a donor, and very supportive of our reasons for delaying the transplant. But one evening we met a friend of my father's who took a different view.

He's a very logical and analytical person and voiced the opinion of many people, when he challenged me, 'But Fran you look so well. Why put your life at risk and have a transplant at all?'

'Because if I don't have a transplant, I'll die.'

'Who says?'

'Everybody, it's plain medical fact, CML kills all patients, usually within five years, unless they have a transplant.'

'But you're still fine. Why do you believe what the medics are telling you when the evidence is against them? I don't understand why you're taking the risk.'

I couldn't think of anything else to say. His words preyed on my mind for ages, and I thought he had a valid point. I only knew I was ill because people told me, I hadn't changed colour or taken to my bed. Maybe he was right? Maybe I shouldn't have a transplant at all?

I talked it all over with Dad who was great. He told me his friend is a very forthright and logical person and he would expect this opinion, but that I shouldn't be swayed by it. Even now I understand where he was coming from, a bone marrow transplant is a weird concept.

My mental clock started ticking a countdown to May 1995. By then Matthew would be two and a half, and Sebastian eighteen months. I felt this was just about old enough for him to know I was his mother and for us to have an unbreakable bond. If he had been any younger when we had a long enforced separation, I would have been terrified of him not recognising me when I came home.

The boys' future nursery schooling was another good reason for delaying transplant. They wouldn't be allowed to come into contact with other children until several months after my transplant because of the high risk of transferring infection to me. After a bone marrow transplant the patient has absolutely no resistance to infection, even less than a new-born infant, and must not have contact with any illness. To minimise risk, anybody who came near me for a year afterwards must stay out of contact with infection. That may delay the boys going to school for twelve months.

When I came home from hospital, Adrian and my parents must stay out of pubs, cinemas and crowded places, and the boys would be banned from contact with other children. That seemed harsh to me, but I knew they would have many years ahead to make up for it, hopefully with me restored to health.

Despite the looming deadline, we had a very happy year as a family, and I treasured every single moment. Many of my friends didn't enjoy their children's baby phase, and I thank God that for me those days were an unconditional blessing. When you're afraid you're going to die, life takes on infinitely more meaning and value, as anyone who faces serious illness will tell you.

But every night I looked at the calendar and tried not to count the days, weeks and months until May 1995. It felt as though there was a bomb in the attic which I knew was there, and couldn't be defused, a bomb that was counting down inexorably to a day when it would blow my happiness apart.

Once my transplant date had been set, it seemed that my life hung by the slenderest of threads. Suddenly I had a deadline, and beyond that a black hole. Adrian and I agreed with my parents that we should have a last family holiday abroad, since I knew I wouldn't be allowed to travel after transplant, even if it went well. I knew many patients who had decided never to travel again, because the risk of picking up infection is far greater abroad.

So we booked a February break in Barbados, the place where Sebastian was conceived, and the six of us had a very precious time together. It was a haven before the storm, I knew – my parents knew – that I knew – I may not make it. So much was unspoken in those last months.

As I lay beside the pool watching my boys play, I realised I was about to risk my life, and this may be my last holiday. Leaving Barbados was the hardest part, I traced my eyes over the island, the sea and the other guests, thinking that I may never look on this scene again. I sat on the plane to come home and tears welled up inside me. I remember choking them so the boys wouldn't see me cry, and so I wouldn't break Mum's heart. Just like the horse chestnut trees at my diagnosis, beauty can be so painful, and life is never more wonderful than when it may end.

Once a date had been set for my admission to the Hammersmith, I was given far more information about the detail of a bone marrow transplant. In my typical style, I demanded to know everything and didn't like what I heard.

Immediately after admission I would be fitted with a *Hickman line* under anaesthetic, which is inserted into the chest to administer drugs directly into my system. Then I would have a programme of chemotherapy and radiotherapy to irradiate and kill my own bone marrow. After total body irradiation I would rest and wait for the awful side effects to begin. These would include loss of the membranes inside the nose, mouth and throat, hair loss, nausea, weakness and immense pain.

Then I would be given the donor's bone marrow by a simple injection, the only part of the procedure which is simple and painless. After transplant I would be closely monitored for positive signs that the donor bone marrow had grafted on to my system, and for negative signs of the life-threatening symptoms of Graft versus Host disease which may include skin problems, nausea, and organ failure. These dangers would remain for a long time after transplant, but are most likely and dangerous in the early stages.

The more I understood, the more afraid I became, but I realised I had no option. While I sat watching *Postman Pat* videos with the boys, as spring turned to summer, my mind would wander over the facts. It was already three years since my diagnosis, and I had played with danger for too long. I kept thinking of Ali McGraw in *Love Story* and remembering her rapid deterioration as leukaemia took hold. I was so afraid, but couldn't talk about it with anyone, not with my parents who were being so brave for me, or with Adrian who was consistently positive and optimistic. So I hid the fears deep inside, and thought some dreadful things which I've never shared with anyone.

Frequently I wondered whether Adrian would marry again if I didn't survive, and how quickly and who too? In my head I listed all our friends and work colleagues and wondered if any of them would become his second wife. It was a painful thought, and I never discussed it with him, but I had the sense to realise that if he found the right girl, it would be infinitely better for the boys to have a step-mother. Private and strange thoughts like these were in my mind far too often and clouded this time before my transplant.

Although Professor Goldman had told me my chance of surviving a transplant was around 45%, I knew that for my family's sake I must go for it believing I would come through. Ahead of me I saw a void. Beyond it was a possibility of a normal future watching Matthew and Sebastian grow up, but I had to pass through the blackness to reach them. Throughout those months I steeled myself to do it. For them, not for myself.

I said a prayer for you today, and know God must have heard,

I felt the answer in my heart, although He spoke no word.

I didn't ask for wealth or fame, I knew you wouldn't mind,

I asked Him to send treasures, of a far more lasting kind.

I asked that He'd be near you, at the start of each new day,

To grant you health and blessings, and friends to share the way.

I asked for happiness for you, in all things great and small,

But it was for His loving care, I prayed the most of all.

Chapter Ten

Wheels in Motion

అ ఎ అ ఎ

From the day they were born, the boys had been at the forefront of our thoughts, plans and hopes. During this time of waiting for my transplant Adrian and I had many conversations with our parents, especially mine who had agreed to take care of the boys while I was in the Hammersmith. I remember one particular occasion in my parents' garden that summer while Matthew toddled around the lawn and forced favourite toys into Sebastian's podgy fists as he sat on his play-mat.

While we drank tea I said to Mum, 'I feel pretty bad about this, because we've landed you and Dad with a huge responsibility.'

'Don't be silly Fran, Dad and I have always said we would look after the boys when you had your transplant. We're lucky to have this time to plan and talk about it, lots of people with leukaemia don't have that time.'

'Do you think the boys will remember me when I come out?'

'Of course they will, the bonds are formed in the first few weeks, and we'll have photos of you everywhere and will talk about you every single day. The boys will paint pictures of what they've been doing and send them to you in hospital.'

I laughed, 'I think you're being a bit optimistic about their talents Mum, but please, please do it for me.'

'And we'll be able to phone and Matthew can talk to you before he goes to bed.'

I yearned for that, but feared for little Matthew's security, 'Not if it unsettles him, however much Adrian and I miss them, it's better than the boys getting upset by hearing my voice.'

'We'll be guided by them Fran. Don't worry.'

'I couldn't do this without you Mum,' I said, fighting back the tears.

'We know Fran, and we do it willingly,' said Mum, in a matter of fact voice, keeping herself together for me as ever.

'About the practicalities' Adrian chipped in, 'Fran and I have been thinking, and we suggest hiring a nanny for the boys while we're in hospital.'

'A nanny? Why do you want a nanny – the boys will be living here with us and Dad and I can manage?'

'We thought it was essential to give you some backup – a nanny could come to your house during the day to spend time with the boys and give you both a break. They can't go to nursery because of the risk of infection, so a nanny could offer a kind of substitute. Then you would have some time off.'

I could tell Dad saw the sense of lightening Mum's workload, so I said to him, 'You two would be a solid rock for the boys, all the time. You would be there day and night instead of us, but a nanny would share the burden. As well as caring for the boys you'll be worried sick about me, which will add extra stress, and you're not spring chickens any more.'

'Oh thanks,' smiled Mum.

'And you'll want to visit me in hospital when it's allowed, and you'd be able to leave the boys with a nanny. We also thought she would be vital when I come home to recuperate. I'll be incapable of doing anything, and house-bound, then Adrian will have to go back to work, so help will be essential until I'm back on my feet.'

There was a pause and Adrian spoke in a quiet voice. 'There's something else we need to say. We have to face the possibility that Fran won't come through. I'm absolutely certain that won't happen, but we need to talk about it. If the worst comes to the worst, I'm going to need a nanny to help me bring up the boys.'

Nobody said a word. All four of us looked at Matthew toddling round the garden with his plastic wheelbarrow. He had filled it with handfuls of soil and leaves. One sock was discarded on the lawn, and his fingers were black. It was a profoundly moving moment, watching the innocence of a child while we discussed a future in which he may lose his mother.

Mum spoke first, 'I understand completely, and I think you should look for a nanny. But whatever happens, you have our one hundred per cent support. Don't they Len?'

Dad didn't look at us, only nodded. I knew he didn't want us to see his face, where pain and grief would be written in his eyes.

Later that week I contacted a local agency and asked for candidates for a nanny's post, assuming I would be inundated with applicants just as they were in Mary Poppins. But the agency supplied details of only four girls and told me there were unlikely to be others.

I received CVs and asked to interview all four. The first three girls didn't seem right for one reason or another, and I began to worry that we would never find the right person. Our situation was utterly different from a normal family, and we were asking for a level of commitment that was quite out of the ordinary. We couldn't risk things going wrong, because the boys would need total stability during my hospitalisation, every factor in our case made it difficult, uncertain and strange. In fact, finding a person prepared to take us on would be a miracle.

When the fourth nanny came to my house for interview I opened the front door and saw an attractive, friendly girl in her twenties, and I thought, 'she's just the sort of nanny I've been looking for.'

But I must have been the most unreasonable interviewer who ever sat in front of an applicant, because I was so difficult to please. As far as I was concerned, Matthew and Sebastian were my miracle boys, and I was over the moon with them in every way. They were my whole life and I hardly dared entrust them to anyone but myself.

It helped a great deal that my parents would be the prime carers of the boys, and as they had brought me up, I thought they could be trusted! If Mum and Dad hadn't been around, I simply couldn't have handed my children over to any nanny because I would have been too afraid she would take my place. My insecurity really manifested itself over this choice.

But Kathryn and I got on well at the first interview. I admired her gentle manner and thought she was a bit like me, which helped in an ironic way.

I told her all about my condition and the planned transplant, and she didn't seem phased. Then I explained our plans for the boys to move in with my parents for the months of my stay in the Hammersmith. 'So initially you would be working for my Mum and Dad at their house, but doing all the things you would normally do here,' I explained.

'What kind of people are your parents?' Kathryn asked.

'Really nice, very easy to get on with and their involvement will actually reduce your workload.'

A shadow passed across Kathryn's face and I guessed she was imagining a couple of dominant grandparents and an old-fashioned regime on their territory. I started to worry that I would never persuade anyone to work for us.

'I know it sounds a bit odd, but you'll like my parents, and obviously you'll want to meet them and see their house before we can make a decision.'

Kathryn said 'Hmmm' and sat quiet and still.

'We thought the nanny could start work here six weeks before my transplant, so she would get to know the boys while I'm still around. That would give stability, and allow them to become settled with a nanny before I disappear. It's very important to me that they don't think their parents have vanished and been replaced by a stranger, but six weeks should be long enough to make you part of their everyday lives.'

'What happens when you come out of hospital?'

'I'll be in a pretty bad way and unable to do anything at first. You would be in sole charge during the day while my husband was at work, then little by little I would be able to do more and get up, but progress could be very slow. I'll find a cleaner to do the housework because I don't expect you to do that.'

Then I tried to explain the after-effects of a transplant as bluntly and vividly as I could.

Her next question shocked me, 'How long will this job last, because I don't want it on my CV that I had a job for only a few months? What if you come home and you're fine and you ask me to move on?'

Maybe I had expected sympathy, but looking back, Kathryn was simply being practical.

'If I make it through the transplant there will be a long recovery period, so even if things go wonderfully well, I'll need you to work for at least a year after transplant. It's never an easy recovery process.'

'What if you go in for your transplant and don't survive?' she asked.

I blinked and stared at Kathryn. The question seemed so easy for her to ask, yet it was a question I had never dared to put to Adrian or anyone in three years. And here it was, hanging in the space between us, as uncomplicated as a request for a cup of tea.

I tried to construct the answer. 'If I don't survive, you'll be needed more than ever, because my husband will have to bring the boys up without me. For the sake of continuity we would want to keep the same nanny, probably for many years. The requirement would be much greater and longer than we originally planned.'

If she was going to be practical, so would I. 'So either way, whatever the outcome of my transplant, you'll have a decent time-scale for a job.'

After Kathryn had left I thought over the interview. On balance I had a feeling she was the right person; young, full of fun, and the sort of down-to-earth woman I could get on with.

I could see the situation from both sides. Kathryn may be worried about the abnormality of the situation, most nannies work for a mother who is at work all day and they have a high degree of freedom. Kathryn was probably afraid that as I would be in the house I'd look over her shoulder and be criticising every move. She may fear my jealousy, knowing I would be shut indoors for months after my transplant, unable to go out for fear of infection.

There were so many unknowns from her point of view, and three key players who would be around her and involved with care of the boys.

From my own perspective, hiring a nanny was a monumental worry in case it didn't work out, and with only six weeks trial period before my transplant, we had no time to get it wrong. What if the nanny resigned half way through? Mum and Dad would be left in charge, and Adrian and I wouldn't even be able to interview replacement candidates.

I pictured myself lying near death in the Hammersmith knowing the nanny had just walked out and I was entrusting the boys to a stranger I had never met. I would be too ill for Adrian to leave me and return to care for Matthew and Sebastian. The worry of it made me cry and have panic attacks. The most important aspect of my treatment was the boys' stability, I thanked God that my parents would be a rock in the storm for them, but I knew the nanny was almost as important.

When Adrian came home I poured out all my worries. He had listened patiently to my assessment of the first three interviews as I described every girl in detail. Now I explained my fear that I couldn't handle a transplant knowing the boys may be left in the lurch.

'Fran, calm down, if we hire a nanny we can put all sorts of safety valves in the contract, saying your medical circumstances call for certain guarantees. We'll speak to the agency about notice terms, and make sure the arrangements are secure. What did you think of Kathryn?'

'I liked her, I think she's the one.'

'At the end of the day I want it to be your decision Fran, you must be absolutely happy about the person we choose. If you like her, ask her to come back and meet the boys with me and your parents.'

I arranged the meeting at my parents' house a few days later and took the boys round for the important first impression. Adrian would join us after work and I felt so sorry for Kathryn, facing the entire Burke and Bevan contingent including two lively toddlers at one fell swoop! But she handled it well.

She had a tour of the house and my parents were relaxed and friendly, then at the end of the meeting we brought the boys in. Until that point we hadn't discussed my illness with them at all, it was totally pointless to try and explain to a one- and two-year-old. So I simply took their hands and said, 'I've got a friend round boys, come and meet Kathryn!' and led them into the kitchen.

They showed very little interest, which was exactly how they treated every adult, and they didn't understand the implications of the situation at all. After Kathryn left, the four of us discussed the meeting in depth. We all felt Kathryn was the right choice, although I wished there had been more applicants to choose from.

'Am I offering her because there's no-one else?' I asked.

'We're choosing her because we get a good feeling about her, and that would be the case if we saw twenty others,' Adrian replied.

So I rang the agency and offered her the job.

I waited nervously for a return call, and when the agency rang they said Kathryn had promised to think about the offer.

This was a shock, and I began to panic in case she turned us down, not knowing where we would look next.

It's human nature that as soon as somebody hints they may refuse you, you want them all the more, and that's what happened over Kathryn. But her request for time was completely reasonable, and I would do exactly the same in her situation, it was a very strange job offer in unique circumstances.

Suddenly I thought of a way of helping her make up her mind. An old school friend of mine lived in the same village as Kathryn, so I rang and suggested she should have a word with Hilary for an honest opinion of me and my family.

I told her, 'I've known Hilary for years and she's a very honest and straightforward person. She will talk to you off the record and be very truthful. She may reassure you we won't be awful employers!'

Hilary had no idea I was looking for a nanny and I didn't prime her. All I know is that Kathryn did bump into Hilary and they did discuss me, and it must have been positive because the agency phoned later and said Kathryn would take the job.

We were very pleased and agreed she would start work six weeks before my transplant in March 1995.

Those first weeks must have been difficult as I was still perfectly capable of running the home and caring for the boys. Kathryn shadowed me to learn how I did things, what Matthew liked to eat, and when Sebastian had his naps. I showed her all their favourite places and taught her our little jokes and special words. In one sense it was light work, but also it must have been a terrible strain for Kathryn, being watched herself and watching me from the sidelines.

But by the time of my admission into hospital, I was confident she knew exactly what the boys needed, and those weeks gave me the confidence I needed before I could say goodbye.

Leading up to the transplant I had lots of cards and good-luck wishes from work colleagues, friends and family, and one Monday morning about a month before my admission, I found a brown paper parcel on my doorstep when I came home after a night away. Inside the brown paper I discovered a beautiful red box, with a label sending me best wishes from Katherine.

I thought 'what's the nanny doing sending me a present? and I opened the box carefully. Inside was an absolutely beautiful silver angel supporting a single candle in her uplifted hands. Adrian looked at the gift and said immediately, 'That's not from the nanny Fran, it's from the Palace!' and sure enough, I saw the mark on the box.

I held my breath as I took in the impact of the gift the Duchess of Kent had sent to prepare me for my transplant. Her letters had explained how she lights candles at important moments, and when she prays.

'Oh my goodness!' I whispered, 'it's been on the doorstep all night!' It was a perfect and deeply significant gift which I still treasure and which came with me to the Hammersmith and stayed by my side throughout transplant. On every day of my stay in hospital, I lit the candle for a few moments, even though naked flames weren't allowed. The nurses used to joke about my secret smoking, and to this day, when I face an important or frightening occasion, I always light a candle in the angel holder and pray one of the many prayers Katherine sent me.

In answer to her request, I let Katherine know my admission date.

Chapter Eleven

Russian Roulette

ॐ ॐ ॐ ॐ

Ever since people had heard about my illness, I had been put in touch with others like me who had leukaemia or related conditions. I developed a small network of people who relied on each other for mutual support. One of the first I met was Libby, who had a bone marrow transplant years ago as Professor Goldman's ninth ever transplant patient. I had contacted her through a mutual friend and she proved to be a role model and source of inspiration. Ever since we met I hoped for a recovery like hers.

There was also Terry Leggett who worked for IBM and who first heard about me through publicity for the bike ride. He had sent me an email explaining that although we'd never met, he also had CML and was waiting for a bone marrow transplant under Professor Goldman at the Hammersmith. We began speaking regularly, swapping stories and sharing the highs and lows of treatment. Even though IBM was a huge company, I was surprised to discover another employee with exactly the same condition, under identical treatment.

But there was one significant difference between Terry and me, I was thirty, and he was in his fifties. Professor Goldman had mentioned the difficulty of treating leukaemia patients who are in late or middle age, and Terry was painfully aware of the dangers. Consultants don't like to go ahead with a transplant after the age of fifty because chances of survival are reduced significantly. Also, donors are not accepted on to the register once they have passed forty, although they may still donate bone marrow until they reach sixty.

Terry and I stayed in touch, and he found a donor in due course and was booked in for transplant. One day, while waiting for my own transplant, I attended out-patients clinic at the Hammersmith and Terry heard my name called out in the waiting room. Without knowing it, we were both sitting in the same room. So Terry introduced himself, and after months of contacting each other by phone and email, we came face to face.

We became good friends. Terry always had a laugh and a joke about his situation and was supremely fit. He regularly went mountaineering, walked huge distances and he was an incredible person. But although he always put a brave face on things, something about his situation always worried me although I couldn't define the cause.

His fitness gave every reason to believe his chances of coming through transplant were good, and I knew he had an excellent donor match because he was lucky enough to have a choice of donors and was able to pick the best.

The last time I saw Terry before his transplant I remember him saying, 'I'm not going round the January sales this year because I won't waste money on a new suit I may never wear!'

Deep inside me his joke hit a raw nerve and I felt uncomfortable.

At my next check-up I asked the staff if I could go to the Dacie Ward to visit Terry who had started his transplant. It wasn't the first time I had visited another patient because we all tended to drop in on friends, and the camaraderie made time in hospital more bearable. But seeing Terry was special because I knew him better than other patients.

When I went into his room he was sitting with his back to me and typing on the computer he had brought from home.

He was surrounded by hundreds of cards including the most enormous get-well card I had ever seen in my life. He was so pleased to see me and so positive that my courage about transplant soared.

Three weeks later, at my next check-up, I again asked whether I could pop down to see Terry. This time, when I knocked on his door, he was lying on the bed while a nurse was putting drugs into his Hickman line. He looked absolutely awful, thin, frail and desperately ill. He just lay on the bed, too weak to get up and whispered words I will never forget as long as I live, 'This is awful Fran, don't do it, whatever happens, don't have a transplant.'

His words were a body-blow, and I had to get out of the ward, for his sake and for my own. I went back to the waiting room and couldn't get the picture of Terry out of my mind. For many days the image of him on the bed and the memory of his words would keep coming back to me.

I said to Adrian, 'I don't think Terry's going to make it.'

Two weeks later I was back in the Hammersmith for another appointment. Although I was dreading seeing his condition, I asked a nurse if I could visit Terry and she disappeared to speak to a sister.

Then, just like the time when they diagnosed my leukaemia in Warwick Hospital years earlier, the sister took me into a private side room. I knew what she was going to say before she opened her mouth. 'I'm very sorry to tell you but Mr Leggett has died.'

I burst into tears before she finished the sentence. This was someone I liked and cared about, and I was simply terrified and grief-stricken. There was so little time until my own transplant and the first person I knew well going through the procedure had failed. It might happen to me. At that time it seemed better for me to go home and abandon the whole idea of a transplant and just take my chance on the amount of life left to me.

During exactly the same period I began a friendship with another leukaemia patient. My brother Nick had heard of a girl with CML who was also under Professor Goldman at the Hammersmith and Nick put us in touch with each other. Her name was Jenny Hamilton from Sheffield and we began a friendship by telephone.

When you have a fatal illness you develop a very deep closeness with people in the same situation as yourself, and bonds form more quickly than they do in everyday life. Jenny and I exchanged tales of each visit to Professor Goldman and found our situations were remarkably alike. Like me she had always been desperately keen to have children, and Professor Goldman had given Jenny three months to conceive a child, just as he'd done for me. But unlike me, she hadn't fallen pregnant before the deadline.

Her time was running out and no donor could be found for transplant so before we met, Jenny had decided to have an autologous transplant with her own cleaned bone marrow. This would rule out the chance of her having a family. Even more sadly, she had relapsed after transplant and Professor Goldman had advised a second attempt.

Jenny went back into the Hammersmith for the repeat transplant and I visited her at my next check-up. I knew she was pretty ill but it was a pleasure to meet her after all the times we had talked over the phone. She was lying on her bed looking very, very sick and her husband was sitting beside the bed. They were a lovely couple and it was so good to be able to comfort her in person, cementing the long-distance concern and care we had developed for each other.

Eventually Jenny came out of hospital and we kept in touch.

On the night before Sebastian's first birthday in October 1994, Adrian and I were at home making a birthday cake for the party next day. Sebastian had developed a passion for his fluffy Tigger, so, although Adrian and I have no experience at all, we made orange icing and as soon as Sebastian was in bed, we began decorating a sponge cake with a picture of Tigger.

But tempers frayed because the icing was drying too quickly and cracking, and our painted black lines wouldn't make anything resembling Tigger. Looking back our efforts seem laughable, Sebastian was one year old and wouldn't even notice the cake, but it was his only birthday before my transplant and I was desperate to make it perfect.

In the middle of the mess, the phone rang and I heard Jenny on the line. 'Hi Fran, I'm afraid I've got some bad news, my leukaemia has gone acute.'

I didn't know what on earth to say to her. We had walked step by step through the last few months and I knew exactly what this meant. We were so similar and had shared so much pain.

'What are you going to do?' I asked.

'I don't know. I don't think there's anything I can do. As far as I know, it's only a matter of time.'

I put the phone down and my world rocked. Nothing made any sense. I stood still and looked at Adrian who was making more orange icing and cursing because he couldn't get it to match the last batch. I felt disconnected from this man with whom I shared my life, and the baby sleeping upstairs with a stuffed Tigger toy. In my pain I actually felt closer to the girl in Sheffield who I had hardly met and who was dying with my illness.

I couldn't finish the cake, and sat lost in thought, dreading the future and grieving for Jenny who meant so much to me. Tears streamed down my face, and for days I kept crying because I knew it was the end. Yet another friend wasn't going to make it, and it seemed I didn't know anyone who had come through.

That was the start of my obsession with the outcome of bone marrow transplant. I decided there weren't going to be any success stories.

Jenny stayed in touch with me throughout my own transplant a few months later and her thoughtfulness was staggering. Despite her own situation she sent me good luck messages, telling me to hang on in there and be strong.

Eventually, months later my brother heard she had died. He kept the news from me for fear of de-stabilising me at a critical time. When eventually I heard the news, I reeled and was even more upset that the news had been withheld. My grief ran very deep.

I want this book to be a tribute to the many people I grew to know and love through my leukaemia and who were claimed as its victims. They are unsung heroes to all but their own loved ones, and I want to honour their memory here. They were much loved and are missed, and their stories prove how great is the need for new donors, and more research into leukaemia.

As soon as my transplant date was scheduled, the Hammersmith put wheels in motion to prepare me for admission. All this went on at the very time when I was struggling to come to terms with my mounting fear that no-one survived bone marrow transplant.

I was invited to the Dacie Ward to spend a day of preparation and receive full details of transplant procedures and meet key staff. My fear of hospitals was as strong as it had been since my experience of X-ray at eight years old when I fractured my elbow. You would think the frequency of my stays in hospital would have made a difference by now, but my childhood panic remained unchanged.

Going to the Dacie Ward for the preparation day was no exception, and I was absolutely terrified. The sister showed me round the ward and to me it seemed as dingy and claustrophobic as a prison. Each patient has an individual isolation room, and there are shared facilities for laundry, guest showers and a little kitchen. The rooms have minimal natural light or views of the outside world, and the whole place smelled of disinfectant and iodine.

We sat with the sister in the day room and she worked her way through a series of questions to determine which named nurse would be assigned to me for the transplant. The intention is to pair you with a nurse who suits your personality to reduce the chance of a clash during what will be a very stressful and painful time.

I sat in the day room thinking 'I don't understand how I'm going to cope in here for so many weeks. I hate this place, I hate everything about it.' My whole attitude was unforgivably negative.

I asked the sister several questions about treatment, and I was particularly bothered about the loss of my hair. 'Does it happen to everyone?' I asked her.

'Absolutely everyone, it's a side effect of chemotherapy and radiotherapy that your hair follicles are temporarily damaged by the radiation.'

'What happens?'

'At first nothing seems to come out, but after a period of days you notice more hairs than usual on your pillow in the morning. Then hair starts to come out in tufts, in the shower, or when you brush it. The loss speeds up and you tend to look rather patchy and thin on top.'

'No, no, I can't bear that, it would break my heart,' I said, clutching Adrian's hand.

'Some patients prefer to shave the head as soon as the tufts start to come out. It's a bit drastic but at least they know what to expect.'

I had already had my hair cut shorter at each visit to the hairdresser for the last year, in preparation for the shock. 'That's what I'm going to do, as soon as I see hair falling out I want you to shave it all off.'

'Gradually hair starts to re-grow, although at first it can be very different from your usual hair. It can be thin or a different colour, but generally it reverts to type several months after transplant. Within a couple of years you should be back to normal.'

Then the sister raised her big issue of concern. It was my biggest fear too.

'In my experience of transplants in mothers who have young children, separation can be very traumatic. I've come to the conclusion that it's actually better for you psychologically and emotionally to take the small risk of having visits from the children, than to have total separation.'

My heart leapt. 'Do you mean I can see the boys?'

'Yes, I do. As long as you can make arrangements to keep them away from all other children, then short visits from them will actually uplift you and help you get through the weeks ahead. But I have to stress that their isolation at home is vital.'

'Yes, yes, thank you,' I whispered. It was one of the most wonderful moments of my treatment.

The final issue the sister raised was my eating pattern. She explained that during transplant, weight loss is unavoidable. Once the chemotherapy and radiotherapy have killed off the tissue lining your mouth and throat, eating becomes excruciatingly painful, and most people find it impossible to continue eating.

She explained 'You are quite small Fran, lighter than we would like, and that puts you at a disadvantage. One of the aspects which determines how long you will stay in hospital is the amount of weight loss. We find that the few patients who manage to keep eating throughout their stay do far, far better than those who have to be drip-fed.

'Once you stop eating naturally you lose your energy and lose the will to get well and go home. At that stage a patient is force-fed on a drip, and one of the side effects is the stomach forgets how to get hungry and eat, so the situation gets worse. A patient who stops eating can lose two, three or even four stones after transplant. From your starting point if you lose even a couple of stone you're going to have big problems.'

'So what are you saying – that I won't pull through?'

'I'm mentioning it now to give you a chance of going home and putting on as much weight as you possibly can. Eat anything and everything that you wouldn't normally have, fat, cream, take-aways, chocolate. It's the very best thing you can do to increase your chance of success.'

The sister told me about Chris Corbin, the famous London restaurant-owner who had a transplant before me and who had continued to eat throughout treatment. He had done phenomenally well and his name was a by-word for the successful transplant outcome. Her advice struck a chord with identical advice I had from Goldman's ninth ever patient, Libby who had always stressed the importance of eating after transplant.

I took the advice very, very seriously and we made a plan that I would start eating for England from that day until transplant. During those months I got my weight up to eight and a half stone which was the heaviest I'd ever been. To this day I'm certain it was a major factor in my survival, and I'm eternally grateful for the advice I was given.

The bomb in the attic of my mind kept ticking and winter turned to spring. Two weeks before my admission I was booked for a pre-transplant session with Professor Goldman and my newly appointed transplant manager Simon Rule. I was really afraid of the visit which made everything seem so final.

The long day consisted of a full schedule of tests and consultations, body X-rays, lung function tests, lumbar punctures and an ECG. I moved from one unit to another to have every part of my body monitored and tested. The data gathered would be used as a base-line for my transplant, against which my deterioration and future progress would be measured.

After tests we were scheduled to meet Simon Rule for a heart to heart interview about doubts, fears and harsh realities.

While we were on the way to see him, I had one of the biggest shocks of my illness. At the first Anthony Nolan reception I had met the young woman called Ellen whose treatment dates had been very close to my own. But she had experienced very problematic Graft versus Host complications after transplant. I believe her GvH was worse than any case Professor Goldman had ever seen, and photographs of her appalling skin and body damage had been used for teaching purposes. After transplant she had been in the Hammersmith for months on end and only recently been allowed home.

On my preparation day I bumped into Ellen and her husband in the corridor. If I hadn't seen her husband I don't think I would have recognised her because of such terrible weight loss.

'Hi!' I hollered, 'how are you?' We always got on well. Then I noticed that Ellen was shaking uncontrollably and coughing. She didn't respond, and I tried again, asking questions and encouraging her. But she didn't recognise me, she was in another world. Her husband behaved perfectly normally and answered my questions and I kept glancing at Ellen, hoping for a glimmer of understanding or recognition. But none came, and she couldn't even speak.

We went into our appointment and I was shaking like a leaf, 'What happened, what's wrong with her?' I kept asking Adrian, full of terror. Maybe the same would happen to me.

Our appointment with Simon Rule was intended to cover the serious side of the future, preparations for the worst, and detail of all aspects of transplant. But I burst into his office and blew his agenda out of the window.

'I can't go through with this,' I said, and started to sob. 'I've just seen Ellen and she's gone to pieces. Is that what's going to happen to me after transplant? Is that how I'm going to end up? Quite frankly I don't even want to try any more if that's what a transplant can do.'

Simon was wonderfully kind and patient. 'No, that's not what is going to happen to you Fran. I can't breach patient confidentiality, but what I can do is reassure you that Ellen's problem is totally unconnected with her transplant. She had other medical problems before she was diagnosed with leukaemia and what you have seen result from those other problems.'

'Why won't it happen to me?'

'Because you have a totally different medical history, we aren't surprised by what has happened to Ellen, and that's all I can say, but you must believe me, her circumstances are unique.'

If only I could have known it then, Ellen was to make a full recovery and is now one of the transplant success stories.

But Simon did reassure me until he could tell I was back on track. 'Are you ready to go ahead now Fran?' he asked.

I replied truthfully, 'As ready as I'll ever be.' And that wasn't saying much.

Chapter Twelve

The Nightmare Begins

ଔ ଋ ଔ ଋ

During the last couple of weeks of freedom, I had my hair cut really short to prepare for the baldness that terrified me so much. I added a couple more baseball caps to my collection, and I determined nobody would ever see me without my hair.

I'd developed a fixation with haircuts at thirteen, shortly after I began going out with my very first boy-friend. My hair had always been long and fair and I loved to hide behind my fringe and tonged side feathers.

For some reason Mum persuaded me to have a change and I agreed with the hairdresser's suggestion to try a layered cut. But I sat in the chair and watched with horror while strands of hair, a full six inches long, dropped onto my shoulders and the floor. When she finished, I had a cropped layered style, with nothing around my face or neck. I screamed and cried and stamped my teenage feet and thought I would never get over it.

And in a sense I never did, because I've been paranoid about having my hair cut for the rest of my life. After the disaster in 1975, I wore a wig and various hats to school, which my friend borrowed to cause great hilarity at the expense of the teachers. I was terrified my boyfriend would dump me, and I vowed never, ever to have short hair as long as I lived. But now, twenty years later, I had no choice.

All the painful memories of being a scalped upper-fourth schoolgirl came back to me as I had my hair cropped before transplant. I had it spikey on top and dreaded coming home.

But Adrian's reaction was as loving as ever, he simply couldn't understand my distress. 'You're about to have a bone marrow transplant Fran, and your hair is the least of your problems. Your hair cut doesn't change anything, and in the scheme of things it's insignificant, you just don't need to be worried about that.'

With Kathryn's help we began to prepare the boys for my admission to hospital. There was no way of knowing how well my transplant would progress, how long I would be in isolation, or when I would be allowed home. We had to plan for the worst, and assume I could be away for months.

We began talking to the boys about mummy going to stay in hospital and they were unconcerned and disinterested. At two and a half years of age Matthew had a tiny glimmer of understanding, but it didn't mean enough to create a reaction. At eighteen months, Sebastian simply sucked Tigger's ears and smiled.

Adrian and I planned their move to live with my parents a few miles away. Over a period of days we moved various items from their own bedrooms to Grandma and Grandpa's house, and talked excitedly to the boys about their good luck in having two new bedrooms.

I was determined to make the transition as gradual and painless as possible, and wanted to avoid a sudden uprooting of all their favourite things. So little by little, we converted my parents' two spare bedrooms into their own, with their mobiles, pictures and teddies. In advance we took over their toy box and helped them select favourite toys and games to 'live' at Grandma's. We took their plastic bikes and paddling pool, and Matthew began to get very excited about the whole exercise. Both boys were fully involved in the process of moving and we let them do lifting and carrying and packing in their own disorganised, clumsy way.

A few key items like duvets couldn't be moved until the last minute, and we decided it was best to let the boys sleep at my parents for my last night, then we would drop in for final goodbyes on our way to London.

On Tuesday 2nd May we packed the car and took Matthew and Sebastian for their first of the many nights they would be away from home. I looked around their new rooms and knew we couldn't have done any better, they were surrounded by everything familiar and loved.

That night our own house seemed very lonely and cold without the boys, and their empty rooms looked ghastly. I wondered if we would ever be reunited as a family inside our own four walls.

The Hammersmith had given me an admission date but warned it may slip by twenty-four hours dependant on a room becoming available, and I prayed and prayed 'Dear God, when I ring let them say I can have an extra day at home!' But when I phoned the hospital on the morning of 3rd May 1995, the office confirmed I should arrive by four o'clock that very afternoon. It was really going to happen, and I felt as cold as steel.

It was a glorious sunny day, and as planned, Adrian and I drove to my parents' house to spend our last few hours with the boys. We had bought presents to make our leaving exciting rather than painful, a plastic work-bench for Matthew because we called him 'Mr Fixit' and a play tent for Sebastian with a tunnel to crawl through. When we arrived, the boys were playing in the garden in their paddling pool, naked, giggling and shrieking. They loved their presents, and the tent was a huge hit.

The whole situation struck me as ludicrous, it was an idyllic family time watching the boys playing, happily oblivious that their mother was about to undergo life-threatening treatment. It was the best and the worst of days rolled into one.

We had a family lunch until we admitted we couldn't delay leaving for London a minute longer.

The farewell with the boys was one of the hardest and worst thing that happened to me throughout my leukaemia. Worse than the diagnosis, worse than labour, chemotherapy, and relapse later. None of the pain and personal grief came close to that goodbye.

My parents were being so brave and strong for me, the boys were blissfully unaware, and Adrian was bottling up all his own pain for my sake. We moved like wooden dolls, getting up from the garden table, walking down the drive, moving mechanistically like puppet characters in a show.

We hugged each other and my parents wished me well, I could see that Dad, the stiff-lipped business-man, was fighting back his tears. He just managed to say the right words that told me he loved me, and I said 'I love you,' and we jumped into the car.

Mum was brilliant, strong as ever, she grabbed Matthew and Sebastian by the hands and said, 'Come on, let's run down the drive and wave them off!' and as Adrian pulled away, Mum and the boys trotted along the grass beside the car. They were so innocent and excited, loving the big goodbye game, it didn't mean an ending to toddlers who had no concept of separation. It meant new bedrooms and presents and fun in the garden with Grandma and Grandpa. I knew their hurt and tears would come later.

I hung out of the car window and waved and watched the three little figures until we turned the bend and they disappeared from sight.

That was it, we reached the M40 island, and my pain suddenly became too much to bear. I had fought my way through four years of sheer bloody hell, through an unnecessary termination of pregnancy, through fear, deaths of friends and hurting the three adults I loved best in the whole world. And now I had lost my precious, precious children, whom I had risked my life to give birth to.

I cried all the way from Warwick to London, helpless, uncontrollable, desperate tears of pain and loneliness. Poor Adrian kept driving and smoothing my knee with his hand,

and telling me how much he loved me and that everything would be all right.

But at the bottom of all my pain was the stark and awful reality, that I was facing a sixty per cent chance I would never return to my home, and never be reunited with my family again.

I arrived at the Hammersmith still in tears, red-faced and more exhausted than I had ever felt.

They admitted me into the Dacie Ward, and I had a burning hot angry rage inside me. All the pain of the journey now turned and focussed on the poor staff and nurses who carried out my admission. I feel very sorry and guilty now, but at the time I didn't care that I was unhelpful and uncooperative. But then something happened to pour healing balm on my aching heart.

The Duchess of Kent had always been very keen to know my admission date, and I hadn't ever wondered why. Without telling me, on the morning of 3rd May she had come to the Dacie Ward in plain clothes, wearing sunglasses and without jewellery, and had scrubbed up in iodine with other visitors, the requirement of ward visiting. No-one had recognised her, the receptionist had no idea who she was and simply told me 'You've missed a visitor who came this morning, but she left some things for you.'

'I can't have a visitor, no-one knows I'm here!' I said.

Adrian was reading the card she had left, 'It's the Duchess of Kent!' he whispered to me.

The receptionist heard him and said 'Oh, I thought she looked familiar!'

I looked at the card, and then at the gifts. Tears sprung readily to my tired eyes as I looked upon the most beautiful bunch of flowers I have ever seen. Suffice it to say that I've hunted florist shops ever since that day to try to find the same flowers. They were sweet peas, and Katherine couldn't have known these are my favourite flowers of all, only prayer could have led to her to choose them. The bunch of gathered stems was a full six inches thick, and the petals were the palest pink of nature's palette, with a hint of deeper pink tracery.

Flowers weren't permitted in the wards and so they stood in beautiful serenity in the washing-room, lending their sweet scent to the iodine-heavy air. I have never found such flowers again, but I won't stop looking.

Katherine had brought other gifts too, wrapped up for me to undo and discover. There was a scented Culpepper cushion in blue and white, and Fred Bear, the most special gift of all. He had a little card attached to him telling me he was her own favourite bear whom she kept in her bedroom. I simply couldn't believe it was real, that she had given away her most precious bear, to me. The note said he had always taken care of her. At that dreadful time, after the most traumatic two hours of my life, Katherine had soothed and helped me.

I thought then, as I was to think many, many times in future, she was an angel in my life, always appearing at precisely the right moment, always giving me the perfect word or gift. The Duchess of Kent is a very prayerful and godly woman, and I'm certain that is what makes her able to reach and touch others in a loving, healing way. This book has been the first time I have been able to explain how much she means to me.

I carried the precious things into my room, number one, Dacie Ward on the ground floor of the Hammersmith. It was the barest, blankest room you can picture. The walls were dingy pink, the window didn't open but looked out onto a brick wall, only inches away from the glass. And I hated it.

We began to unpack immediately, and Adrian busied himself setting up our home computer, beside the hospital TV and video. My parents had arranged for a telephone line to be put into the room so we could talk to the boys every night, and it was to become my lifeline. We covered as much of the walls as we could with pictures and get-well wishes. I set up my ghetto blaster and put our clothes in the cupboard, and then I was overwhelmed with a burning desire to get out. Anywhere, to the hot London streets, or anywhere but that prison. I didn't feel ill, I was fine, and wanted to escape.

A nurse appeared with a pot of four different drugs which she insisted I must take. I was still paranoid about tablets of any kind, and bitterly resented the hospital for forcing these on me so soon. I insisted on knowing exactly what I was taking, and what each drug would do. It's probably a good thing no-one mentioned that in three weeks time I would be swallowing thirty-six tablets a day, on top of an entire programme of intravenous drugs.

The nursing staff subjected me to more tests and indignities, and my anger against the medical world hadn't subsided. I was even crosser when they told me my named nurse was away on holiday until the following day. A young nurse stuck swabs up my nose and in my armpits, took blood, weighed me and wrote everything down.

For years I had felt like an object of interest to the medical profession, they loved to measure every part of my anatomy, make notes, and debate what they found. In the hot anger of that afternoon, I felt a searing resentment that no-one was measuring the progress of my heart, the rips and tears of it breaking into pieces. They prodded and poked me and expected me to carry on smiling, but that day, I dropped the mask of politeness and let my pain show.

When the tests were complete the nurse said, 'We'll begin your chemotherapy and radiotherapy in a few days time, and while it's killing everything off, you'll still have an immune system. That means for the first week or ten days before your bone marrow transplant, you won't be in isolation and can still go out. The length of time varies, but we'll be monitoring your white cell count, and while it still exists, you have protection against infection.'

She turned to Adrian, 'I advise you to take Fran out in-between treatments and buy her lunch and dinner every day. Once the door shuts and isolation begins she will be on a very strict diet and the food will be limited. Make the most of the next few days.'

'Does that mean I can have visitors until then?' I pleaded, thinking of the boys.

'Certainly, while you still have a white cell count. We'll give you warning before isolation begins.'

My spirits soared as I realised I could have an early visit from Matthew and Sebastian. Suddenly things didn't seem quite as bleak, the smallest unexpected pleasure can make all the difference when you're at rock bottom.

'Well I think that's everything,' said the nurse, closing her files.

'Can we go out now?' Adrian asked.

'Sure.'

You couldn't see me for dust, I was out of the ward within seconds.

We found a Chinese restaurant and I ate an obscene amount of food, in a last ditch attempt to gain weight before transplant.

Food became a very important part of the next few days, and I can remember every meal out. We almost went broke eating in London! The next day we had lunch in Ealing Broadway and spent ages in Marks & Spencer with the hospital diet sheet, working out what I would be allowed to eat once I was in isolation.

The Dacie Ward had a tiny kitchen with a microwave where Adrian would be allowed to prepare and heat meals to tempt me into eating after transplant. The diet sheet was very strict, and banned many ingredients and food types. But we walked up and down the food hall listing foods that met all three criteria, I liked them, thought I might fancy eating them, and they were permitted by the hospital.

Every morning we walked to the hospital canteen and ate a full English breakfast. It got harder, but I forced myself to eat as much as possible.

The situation improved next day when my named nurse Kath arrived. I liked her as soon as she walked into my room, agreeing she had been well-matched to me. I knew we would get on famously, and felt more settled now I had a single point of contact. The named-nurse relationship is important because you spend so much time together in a very confined space.

Kath began a series of tests in earnest to provide normal levels against which every body function would be compared after transplant. She gave me lots of tablets to prepare me for chemotherapy and transplant, and Adrian took everything in and wrote copious notes in his book.

That night my brother Nick took us out for dinner at Gary Rhodes' *Greenhouse* and we had a wonderful meal together. Nick brought a giant *Paddington Bear* to cheer me up in hospital, and I ate even more than the night before. We stayed out so late that the entire hospital was locked, and the only way in was through Casualty. That night was so much fun, I almost felt normal.

I had dreaded Friday – the day my *Hickman line* was scheduled to be fitted. During a bone marrow transplant you have so many intravenous drugs and blood tests, that your veins wouldn't stand up to the battering, so a *Hickman line* is fitted into the chest by surgical procedure.

It is routed between the ribs and inserted without general anaesthetic, not a pleasant procedure, and you are given heavy sedation to help with the pain. But I had decided to be stubborn, and as my full treatment didn't begin until the following Monday, I had been given permission to go home at the weekend to see the boys. So on Friday afternoon I wanted to visit the Disney store on Regent Street to buy them both a little present. I wouldn't be well enough for shopping if I was under heavy sedation, and insisted on having the *Hickman line* fitted without it.

I'm sure I don't need to spell out that my idea turned out to be very foolish, especially as I was dreading the pain. The nurses tried to persuade me to have sedation in the morning, thinking I could sleep it off all afternoon, and I steadfastly refused.

'No, you don't understand, I have to go out this afternoon,' I insisted, determined to buy the boys a treat.

I trundled along to theatre to have the line fitted, and it proved to be a dreadful ordeal. Despite the local anaesthetic, I was fully aware, and could feel what was being done to my chest. It takes a lot of force to separate the ribs and fit the three tubes behind the lungs and into the heart. And I was afraid of the machines hemming me in from above, from which the consultant operated instruments by keyhole surgery while peering into a monitor. When he had finished, I had three pipes coming out of my chest, one to put drugs into me, one to take blood out, and one spare.

I knew the line would make the rest of my treatment more bearable, and in retrospect it was one of the best things I ever did, but having it fitted wasn't a good experience.

Immediately after insertion you have to be X-rayed to make sure the lung hasn't been pierced, as the line passes very close to the lung to reach the heart. I remember standing in X-ray feeling giddy, then fainting from the ordeal without sedation. The nurses wheeled me back to my room on a stretcher and told me to rest.

Unbelievably, after an hour in bed, I announced I felt better and said 'Right! Let's go shopping!'

Adrian and I took a taxi to the Disney store and bought Tigger dungarees for Sebastian and a Mickey Mouse cap for Matthew. I didn't feel well, but the thought of giving the treats to the boys kept me going. It was a rather drastic case of shopping therapy.

The next day was a wonderful and unexpected highlight, Adrian was allowed to drive me home to my parents and spend a night with the boys. Again we found them playing in the paddling pool, and we were overjoyed to see each other.

My close friend Dee had asked whether she could pop over to discuss something important. She walked into the garden, hugged me and got straight to the point, 'I've had an idea – I'm going to shave my head before you come out of hospital, so we'll be bald together. If there are two of us without hair, no-one can look at you and wonder what's the matter with my friend. I'm hoping to get people to sponsor me to raise money for Anthony Nolan. What do you think?'

I was completely taken aback, Dee knew how much the loss of my hair terrified me.

She went on, 'I've already discussed it with my hairdresser and he's told me all about re-growth and what it will look like.'

I was profoundly touched that Dee cared enough to do this for me, just because I was so afraid, but said, 'I can't let you Dee, it's a lovely thing to offer, but you really mustn't. It's good enough for me that you'll be there when I've got no hair, and if you're walking around bald too, I'm going to carry a huge heap of guilt about it.'

I hope I didn't hurt her feelings, but I simply couldn't let her do something that would have worried me so much.

Then came the moment I had dreaded – for Dee to leave. We had made a pact that when we parted for the last time before my transplant, we would never say goodbye. Dee hugged me and said the words we always spoke, 'See you later.' We were both fighting back tears.

'Yep, see you later,' I replied, and let her go. I watched her car drive away until the bend in the road hid her from sight.

On Sunday morning we had to face another goodbye with the family and travel back to London for the next stage of treatment. Although I hadn't expected it, the Hammersmith wanted to begin my chemotherapy that day. We were totally unsure what to expect.

Chemotherapy turned out to be huge bags of liquid that were delivered to my room, hooked up on the drips, and delivered through my *Hickman line*. Each bag took several hours to dispense into my blood. In conjunction with the radiotherapy, it would kill off my own immune system and my body membranes.

It continued for several days and the hospital agreed I could have a family visit. Staff were always one hundred per cent cooperative with personal requests. Whenever Adrian and I asked to go out or to have a visit, the nurses fitted my treatment around our schedule. On the Wednesday, a week after my admission, they gave my chemotherapy early in the morning so Mum and Dad could bring the boys and take us out for lunch while my appetite remained intact.

We were overjoyed to see Matthew and Sebastian, although they seemed shy and reserved in the strange environment. My heart went out to the poor little mites, who were far too young to understand what hospital meant.

We went to a family pub for lunch and then to Kew Gardens because I wanted to be in healthy outdoor places, where I was less likely to pick up any infection before transplant. We ambled along the river and watched a university rowing tournament, and life felt almost normal, although I yearned to jump in the car and go home with the boys. It was very hard to say another goodbye.

Next day my radiotherapy began, and again, I wasn't fully aware of the procedure. First the team came to my room and measured every part of my body. Using a tape measure they recorded the length and diameter of my arms, neck, legs and head, to prepare the radiotherapy unit for me.

After that I walked to the unit and was invited to choose a tape or CD to play during treatment. There wasn't an extensive choice and I selected *Dirty Dancing, The Time of my Life,* rather an ironic selection in the circumstances.

I was admitted to the radiotherapy room and lay down while staff placed packs over various body organs for protection. I was told I must not move at all, under any circumstances, no matter how much I itched.

And then I lay still, for a long time, knowing my body was being zapped by lethal rays that would kill my ovaries, my body tissues, and my leukaemia. All the time I listened to *The Time of my Life,* thought about what was happening to my body, and worried about the future.

Now, whenever I hear the song, it takes me back to my three days of radiotherapy and I can actually relive the sensation and emotions of that time. It was a strange period between health and sickness, between my old world and the next. I was stepping out in faith and letting the medical profession do terrible things to me in the name of healing. I shuddered to think about what would happen if they got it wrong.

Chapter Thirteen

No Going Back

৬ ৯ ৫ ৯

I t is very difficult for me to write this part of my story, for a number of reasons, not least the feelings of other families and patients. But to leave out this chapter would be an injustice to those who have lost the fight against leukaemia.

In the week of waiting for my transplant, between chemotherapy and receiving my donor marrow, three patients in the tiny Dacie Ward died. There were ten beds on the ward, and in one week, three people didn't make it. Very soon after admission I worked out the procedure when a death took place.

Staff would walk along the corridor, closing doors and blinds and calling out to patients to stay in their rooms for five minutes. They wanted to protect us from the terrible sight of a body being wheeled away.

The first time it happened I peeped out from behind the blind on my glass door and I saw the image which came to terrify me more than any other. A metal trolley, a white sheet, a person who could be me.

I knew there was a young girl next door to me, now in isolation, and whom I'd seen when I was admitted. She had looked so ill, and the image of her face stayed in my mind. I had longed to know her, but she died that week. Then a little boy died too.

I freaked out with the pain and fear of it. I could hear relatives weeping and doors banging, and I pictured the same scene being played out over my own body, maybe in a few weeks time. It was too much for me.

After the third death, I begged Adrian to fetch Simon Rule, my transplant manager, to my room.

Simon came in and couldn't have been more sympathetic. He closed the door and gave me his full attention.

'Simon, I've got to know why each of the three patients have died this week, please tell me.'

'You're not even supposed to know that any patients have died Fran, we try to shield you from that.'

'You can't pull the wool over my eyes. Of course I know. Why have they died? Were any of them like me? That's three in ten, thirty per cent in a week – I have to know why Simon.' I was visibly shaking.

Without breaking a single confidence, and telling us no personal detail, Simon explained the differences to my own case. I kept glancing at Adrian to see how he was responding, and as usual, Adrian understood every aspect of the medical detail and I relied on his reaction to see whether it was OK.

'Fine, that's fine,' Adrian said to Simon, and I felt a wave of relief. Then Adrian turned to me, 'It's OK Fran, your case isn't like any of the other three. There's no reason to be afraid.'

Simon left us and I felt thankful for his concern. He never lost his patience with me, even when I bombarded him with unreasonable and intense questions.

I had to know the facts, it's part of my personality, I am never the ostrich, burying my head in the sand and hoping the problem will go away. I want to know what I'm facing and how bad the worst can be.

Adrian understood how I ticked, and knew what to say. 'It's a case of statistics Fran, some people who have a transplant will die, and that's a fact. This is going to sound very callous and I don't mean it to be, but if statistics say a certain percentage of people die in transplant, then this week, statistically it's less likely to be you.

'Nothing will take away the pain of bereavement of other families, but you're facing the biggest challenge of your own life and you need to be positive. Keep your spirits up, and believe you are going to be one of the fortunate ones.'

Then I came upon an article about the success-rates of transplant being largely dependant upon donor type. For my case, the article was bleak and terrifying in its scope. It said the ideal donor was a young male, but if it was a female, transplant works better if she has never had children. All I knew about my donor was that she was female, my age, and had children. This was the worst news in the world at the worst of all possible times. I was trapped in my isolation room facing new information that changed the way I thought about my donor.

When I saw Professor Goldman, I begged him to be honest.

'I'm giving you a forty/sixty chance Fran, that's a forty per cent likelihood of you coming though. For your type of leukaemia that's pretty good.'

'It doesn't sound good to me. Is my donor a good enough match?'

'As I've said before, not good, but not bad.'

'How can I risk my life for that! This article says I would be better with a young male, and that's not what I've got.'

'If you want me to be honest, I will be. Over the many years I've carried out bone marrow transplants, more and more of them have been successful. I would say your chance is actually nearer to forty-five per cent than forty. But within that bracket there is a chance of surviving with a reduced lifestyle, with things like organ problems. But you have to face the fact that this transplant was your only option, without it you will certainly die, probably sooner rather than later. You have one donor match and it's strong enough.

'There are a lot of factors in a successful transplant, many we don't understand. But you have age, general health and fitness on your side, and you have a lot of supporters, not least of whom are your sons. They are a heck of a reason to survive. I'm sorry this isn't a more exact science, but we're doing our best for you.'

'Thank you,' I said, knowing that even as we spoke, the chemotherapy and radiotherapy were killing my body cells. It was far too late to turn back now, the choice was already made.

After this conversation, I said to Adrian, 'I've just realised what a transplant is, it kills you so you can live, literally and metaphorically, at this moment, I'm dying to live.'

My transplant of donor bone marrow had been scheduled for 12th May. All that day I was impatient and kept asking my nurse Kath 'Has it arrived yet?' At least once every hour, I popped my head out of my door and asked for news.

'Be patient Fran, it's on its way,' Kath told me.

The marrow arrived on the ward late in the afternoon, and I was overjoyed to know it was there, safe, real, hope-giving.

I rushed out into the corridor to ask if I could see it, saying aloud, 'Yes, yes, it's here, brilliant!' and wondered why everybody was so quiet. The nurses were absolutely silent. And then I saw why, in a room off the corridor a little boy had died only a few moments earlier. His family was sitting around the bed, weeping uncontrollably. Then they walked past me, and I stood watching the sad procession of those for whom life and hope had died forever.

The elation of my moment had vanished utterly and I stood, as empty and cold as I have ever felt. Suddenly it wasn't a time for joy, but for the gnawing of secret fear and grief.

At every single anniversary of my transplant I remember that little boy, he will always stay in my memory, etched there by pain as the one who lost the fight on my special day. I pray his parents have found peace at last.

A nurse ushered me back into room one, and I was quiet and numb. The donor marrow arrived in a drip bag and I remember being amazed there was so much of it.

Kath hooked the precious bag up onto the drip and a doctor whom I'd never met came into my room. Immediately I panicked. 'Hi, why are you here?' I asked, suspecting the worst.

While Kath hooked the bone marrow supply into my *Hickman line* he explained, 'I'll sit with you throughout the first hour of transplant to monitor things. Often, if there are going to be problems, there's a bad reaction within the first hour, and we want to pick up the very earliest signs. So it's a safety precaution and we do it for everybody.'

After days of nasty treatments, receiving bone marrow was actually painless and easy. It took between four and five hours for the entire bag to drip into my system, and I felt not a jot different. I still felt quite well, and it was no more disconcerting than a blood transfusion, although it was a surreal experience, receiving into my body a product which would either kill or save me. I don't say cure, you are never cured of leukaemia.

While it happened, Adrian and I talked about the momentousness of what was happening in my body. We bitterly regretted forgetting our camera, and a nurse kindly offered to lend us a disposable camera to record the occasion. The treasured photo now hangs in pride of place at our home.

The transplant began at six in the evening on 12th May, and we would come to celebrate that day as my new birthday. The medics call it day zero, and the next is day one. Every test and count after transplant is recorded on the number of the day since receiving donor marrow, and it seems very appropriate to name the day my life began again as day one.

The treatment had irradiated my bone marrow, and my own white cell count was falling toward zero, exactly as planned. From day one, every test result is scrutinised for a presence of new white cells. It's a waiting game, and even a count of 0.001 would be cause for great celebration – proving that the donor's marrow had begun to generate brand new white cells in my body.

I had a relatively peaceful sleep with Adrian on the camp bed that he set up beside me each night. When I woke and felt afraid, I reached out for his hand.

Next morning my blood test proved I still had a white cell count, so the chemotherapy and radiotherapy hadn't yet finished killing everything off.

One of the first things I did was to telephone the Anthony Nolan Donor Welfare Officer, the wonderful Marjorie Gordon-Box, to pass a thank you on to my mystery donor. All donors are assigned a welfare officer who takes care of them and ensures the patient and donor have no way of getting in direct contact.

When Marjorie answered the phone I said, 'I'm absolutely thrilled that my donor went through with it, how is she?'

'I visited her this morning and she's fine, but I don't think she's going to get much rest, her children are bouncing off the walls!'

Immediately I had a mental picture of a lovely family-centred woman, and liked her all the more. 'I want to send a card and a bouquet of flowers to her to say thanks. Can you organise it, because you know where she is?'

Marjorie sounded surprised, 'Oh, I'm not sure, but I'll talk to her and get back to you.'

I could tell Marjorie didn't want to encourage even indirect links between me and the donor, which was very wise, in case I didn't pull through.

Marjorie knew what I didn't, that my donor was in a London clinic only a few miles away from the Hammersmith, resting after giving bone marrow from her hip, while her husband and children were staying in a local hotel.

I was intrigued by every little snippet of information I gleaned about my donor, and was sure she was a family person, just like me. I longed to meet her and pestered poor Marjorie on the phone about the thank-you flowers. 'Have you spoken to my donor yet?'

'I have, and rather than flowers, she says she would love to have a picture.'

'Anything, absolutely anything,' I said, 'I'll get her a picture.'

'Well, it's not just any picture, she would like a copy of the one that's hanging on the wall of her room at the clinic. It's a famous painting of a woman with children in a field full of poppies. Your donor says she imagines the woman as you.'

'Will you speak to the hospital for me and ask them how much money they want for that print? Please tell the hospital I've got to have it, I don't mind how much it costs.'

Marjorie's negotiations must have been successful, because only days later, she told me she had presented the picture to my donor, and I listened with avid fascination, 'Your donor told me every time she looks at the painting at home, she will think of you.'

'When can I meet her?' I asked Marjorie.

'At least a year after transplant Fran, probably longer, that's the rule, and you'll have to be patient.'

Day One of my new life was a Saturday, and my nurse said that as I had a residual white cell count, the boys could make another visit. I was as excited as a child while we waited for my parents to arrive at the Hammersmith.

Mum had dressed the boys in their cutest outfits and I wanted to squeeze them for ever. I knew she was anxious to show me they were being looked after just as I would have done myself.

We took a taxi to the *Intercontinental* for lunch and the boys squeaked with excitement at their first London cab ride. They pressed the buttons and flipped the seats up and down and I couldn't take my eyes off them. At the hotel, a delicious buffet was laid out, but since chemotherapy, my food restrictions banned me from eating anything that had been sitting at room temperature. There was always a danger the food may have been touched or contaminated by flies or bacteria. The hotel prepared a special fresh meal from the kitchen, and I felt very awkward for causing a fuss.

We really enjoyed being with the boys, but at the same time it was immensely frustrating, knowing we could only hold them for a moment before they would be whisked away again.

All too soon the time came for them to leave, and when Mum called the boys, Matthew suddenly became hysterical. In the middle of my room at the Dacie Ward he screamed and held on to me saying 'I'm not going to leave Mummy.'

He had been apart from me for too long, and he must have feared I was never coming home. It was a terrible moment watching him go crazy.

'Come on, I'll walk with you to the car,' I said, taking his hand.

All the way out of the building he stamped and dragged his feet as only a two year old can, and when we tried to put him into his car seat he went as rigid as a board. He was truly hysterical and it was breaking my heart.

Once we had strapped him in he screamed as if he were being murdered, 'Mummy. Mummy, don't leave me, I want to stay with you!'

I was in bits, falling apart myself to see him that way.

My parents were wonderful and told me what I needed to hear, 'Don't worry, as soon as the car pulls off he'll be fine, he will stop crying immediately and fall sound asleep.'

In my heart I knew they were probably right, but my emotions were in tatters and the episode de-stabilised me. As the car pulled away, Adrian and I waved and I could see Matthew's fingers scratching at the side window, trying to get through to me.

Adrian hugged me as we walked back to my room and I was sobbing uncontrollably, saying, 'How can I have done this to our children? How can I have left them, it isn't right, I'm destroying them.'

I couldn't be consoled, and the nursing team tried talking to me and soothing me but nothing, and nobody could help. I kept seeing the image of Matthew's scratching fingers, and hearing him call for me.

Staff were genuinely worried, and in the evening one of the nurses came to me and asked, 'Would it help if we managed to let you out for a few hours tomorrow so you can go home and see the boys in their home environment? We think if you could see them being normal and happy, it may build you up for the separation you've got to endure over the next few weeks. We don't want your last meeting before isolation to be so painful, we'd like you to have a positive few hours with them.'

I dried my tears with gratitude for this supreme thoughtfulness, and said I would like to do what the nurse suggested. Then my mother rang from her mobile and told me Matthew had fallen asleep only half an hour after they left. 'Listen, I'm ringing from the car and there's no screaming. He's sleeping peacefully, just as I said he would.'

The nurses worked out all the timings for Day Two so I could have my drugs early and late in the day and be released for a few precious hours.

The next morning, with great trepidation, Adrian drove to my parents for lunch. We would be with the boys from eleven until three. When we walked into the house, I couldn't believe my eyes. Matthew was playing as happily as a sand-boy, giggling and busying himself. You wouldn't have believed he was the same child as the hysterical boy of twenty-four hours earlier. My parents, in their maturity, had been right – he didn't have a problem. Even when it came to the time for us to leave, he hugged me and was perfectly happy to let me go.

It did me a lot of good to see the children happy in their new home environment, and a peace descended on me to replace the anguish of the previous day. It was an important step just before my isolation began.

The very next morning the sister popped her head around my door and said, 'Adrian, I think you should take Fran out for a big lunch, because this may be your last time before isolation begins. We haven't had the blood test results back yet, but if the white cell count has dropped you'll be in total isolation and this door will shut. So make the most of it and go out while you still can.'

We went to Ealing Broadway and shopped for a present for my father's birthday which would be celebrated while I was in isolation. Then we went to lunch and for the very first time in months, when my meal came to the table, I thought 'crikey – I'm not hungry!' The chemotherapy and radiotherapy had started to affect my appetite at last. Until that day I had continued to eat really well and my weight was still rising slowly.

'The drugs must be taking effect,' I said to Adrian, 'I don't feel right at all.'

'Do you feel ill?'

'No, not exactly, it's weird, I don't feel like myself, and I don't want any food. Something is happening to me, I guess it's all starting.'

'Don't worry about your lunch, just leave it Fran.'

I tried two mouthfuls and couldn't swallow. It was to be the start of the horrible slide downhill.

As soon as we returned to the Dacie Ward the sister popped her head around my door.

'Well that's it Fran. Your white cell count has dropped below one, and you're in isolation from this minute. If I had seen your test result earlier, I would never have let you go out. From now on this door must stay closed at all times and you never leave this room.'

She smiled and closed the door to the world.

'Well I guess that's it,' I said to Adrian.

Chapter Fourteen

Rock Bottom

ଔ ଛ ଔ ଛ

As soon as the door banged shut, I was aware of a strange and new silence. Until that moment I had kept my door open, to emphasise my last taste of freedom. So I had become immune to the noises of a busy hospital, the squeaking trolley wheels, metal implements clattering on metal trays, and the dinner and drug rounds being delivered.

Now an eerie silence settled on the room, and for a while, Adrian and I didn't know what to do. I realised I couldn't even put my head outside the door until or unless my new bone marrow accepted my body and began to produce white blood cells inside me. The significance of the moment was awesome.

Adrian spoke to my parents and they discussed the total isolation programme which must now begin for the boys. From now on when the nanny took them to the park she could only take the boys out of the car if there were no other children about. No more parties or friends to play. I was so worried and hoped this time of withdrawal wouldn't damage them in the long term.

Adrian sat down on the bed and I looked around my room afresh. How I had hated it on arrival a fortnight earlier, but now I accepted, almost liked it. The square pin-board was covered with good luck cards three or four deep, and paintings from the boys. On the bed was today's post, which

I tore open with eager fingers, grateful that every single day throughout my stay I received notes and cards and letters from friends.

At admission I had the standard lecture about receiving post, which I was allowed to open if I washed my hands immediately afterwards. If a letter fell on the floor, I couldn't open it at all.

Today I found a smart envelope and guessed it was from the Duchess. Inside I found another beautiful prayer card, written in her own hand in beautiful script saying she would visit the very next day, as ever with perfect timing.

We had spoken several times on the phone since my admission and Katherine had been determined to visit me, although I confess I never thought she really would. But now her visit was definite, I began to worry about the practicalities. It was to be a private, unannounced visit, and I guessed that if the consultants and doctors knew she was coming, they would whisk her off to promote their facilities and laboratories and force her to assume her professional role.

I talked it over with Adrian and we decided to say nothing to anybody about her visit, and just hope nobody recognised her, as they hadn't the first time. We didn't want any fuss, and neither did Katherine.

Then I worried about how she would find her way to my room, so we agreed to mention the visit at the last moment to the ward sister. Adrian explained to her, 'The Duchess of Kent is coming to see Fran shortly and she doesn't want anyone else to know. It is a small, low-key visit, so is it possible for you to keep a look-out, and when you see her washing her hands in the gowning-up room, just show her the way to Fran?'

'Yes, of course, I'll keep it very quiet.'

'Please,' I begged, 'I have promised her.'

The sister was as good as her word, and soon afterwards she reappeared with my visitor, who was wearing sunglasses, the obligatory apron and smelling of the compulsory iodine wash. From now on, every person I was permitted to see, would dress and smell exactly the same.

But despite the apron, Katherine looked like an angel. She took off her glasses to say hello and under the hospital apron she was wearing very plain, casual clothes, a long skirt and polo-necked jumper, as if she shopped in an everyday department store. But her simple beauty transcended her outfit, she possesses a serenity and loveliness which come from within.

We had just begun to talk, when there was a knock at the door and the sister reappeared. I was terrified she was bringing a stream of interested staff, but she didn't. 'I think you left this in the gowning-up room,' she said, holding up a handbag and leaving at once. We laughed with the Duchess, the ice was broken and we had a perfectly wonderful time together.

I never, ever thought a member of the Royal Family would come to visit me, and I was over the moon to see her. The attention and concern made me feel very special and the visit meant so much.

The next few days were very strange, I hadn't yet begun to feel awful, and didn't want to lie in bed. So I passed the time watching videos and listening to music and Adrian kept himself cheerful and busy.

One day my brother Nick came to take Adrian out for a drink, they weren't supposed to go into pubs, and if Adrian went anywhere busy or smoky he had to strip and change before he could come back into my room.

He enjoyed playing golf at the public driving range in Ealing, and came back full of news and funny stories to amuse me.

Most of Adrian's time was taken up in food shopping, laundry and working on the computer. He did the laundry for both of us, and stocked the fridge in our room with little treats for himself, of wine, beer and chocolates. Often our nurse would pop in at the end of her shift and have a glass of wine with Adrian, to keep him company, while I chatted and laughed with them. I was really happy to see him busy and still able to socialise, which would help him get through the long days ahead.

Once isolation began, his biggest hobby was working on our home computer. Adrian had always been very well-informed about my case and drug treatments, and decided to record every step of my progress since transplant on the PC.

He began to produce computer-generated graphs of every aspect of my case, my weight, white cell count, blood, haemoglobin cells, and platelets with a separate graph tracking each factor. If something could be monitored, he produced a graph, printed it off and stuck it with others all over the walls of my room.

One day, before I became seriously ill, the transplant manager came into my room on a tour of the unit introducing a new member of the management team. Immediately the new man said, 'Wow, I think it's fantastic that the Hammersmith produce all these graphs of patients' progress!'

Simon Rule replied with a hint of embarrassment, 'Actually, these aren't produced by the hospital, they're created by Adrian – he's rather keen on it!' We all laughed and Adrian got a name for himself as the graph wizard.

It was a sobering process watching everything fall, my white cell count, haemoglobin and platelet levels all dived as the chemotherapy and radiotherapy continued to do their work.

I knew the donor marrow was inside me, finding its way into my own bone, and I prayed every day that it would accept me and begin to manufacture new white cells. Unless it did that, I would die.

Every day, on his morning round, Simon Rule examined me for the first dreaded signs of Graft versus Host disease. For some reason, skin changes can be detected earliest on the soles of the feet and palms of the hands. So every day he checked mine. He and his band of merry men, as I called them in my head, would gather around my bed to watch him check me. I felt like an animal in a zoo.

A few days later, the thing I dreaded most began, I found lots of hairs on my pillow when I woke up. The next day was undeniably worse and if I pulled hard, clumps of hair came out in my hand.

On May 19th, day seven, I woke and said to Adrian, 'That's it, my hair's got to go. I'm going to have it shaved today.'

'OK love, whatever you think,' he said.

As soon as Kath appeared for her first call of the day, I begged her to shave my head. Sadly, she fetched clippers and did as I asked, and I watched with horror as my full head of hair fell onto the floor. I felt indescribably sad, and it was one of the least painful, but most terrible aspects of my entire treatment.

Kath was brilliant. 'Right, that's done,' she said, 'I'm going to leave you alone together to have a chance to get used to it. I won't come back or give you any treatment for the next hour.'

As soon as Kath left us I went straight to the mirror and burst into tears. Adrian held me and as long as I cried, he wouldn't let me go. Over and over he said the words I needed to hear, and which were utterly sincere, 'It's not important Fran, what matters is that you live. Your hair will grow back and I still love you, you're still Fran to me, I don't see you any differently without hair.'

He couldn't have been more supportive, and even though it was a matter of desperate importance to me, Adrian genuinely didn't mind me being bald.

Once my tears subsided he asked me to get out the entire collection of baseball caps I had been storing up. There were freebies, ones advertising sports, American and gaudy ones, the entire collection strung up around my room. One by one I tried them all and worked out which I could bring myself to wear.

My biggest worry was for the boys, that they would be shocked and horrified to see me bald, perhaps even fail to recognise me. But of course, children are much more resilient than we give them credit for, and the first time they saw me, neither of them seemed concerned.

I also worried my parents would disapprove of my decision to shave rather than go bald slowly. But I had weighed up the pros and cons and decided my new hair would look far better growing back if it all began from the same even start.

From that moment I was never seen without a baseball cap, I wore one from waking until falling asleep at night. Some people look good without hair, but I can honestly say I'm not one of them!

From that time I began to feel poorly and found it increasingly difficult to reply to my letters or speak on the phone, so Adrian did it for me. I began to feel nauseous and started to wear an anti-travel-sickness wrist-band which helped considerably.

The problem was made much, much worse by the thirty-six tablets I needed to swallow each day. By this stage I developed what is known as the gag reaction, and vomited every time I took a tablet. This led to a phobia where I could be sick even before I tried to swallow a pill. The staff attempted to give me as many drugs as possible in liquid form, but very quickly the awful taste also made me vomit. I was very sick indeed and the nurses attempted to give me all drugs intravenously through my *Hickman line*, although some still had to be taken by mouth. The reaction to my drugs was yet another indignity and cause of pain.

As I declined, Adrian became busier, and spent more and more effort shopping for food to tempt me into eating. He hated leaving me, and was as quick as possible whenever he drove to *Marks & Spencer* to choose soft foods that we had decided in advance met the criteria – permitted and tasty.

When he returned to the ward, Adrian heated my food in the patients' microwave and tried to persuade me to eat. I listened with fascination as he told me about a patient in a nearby room who insisted on eating the hospital food. At that time it was dreadful, one of the reasons why the Hammersmith is now involved in a huge fund-raising campaign to build a new unit with a new hospital kitchen.

By Day Nine I started to feel very, very sick. I was weak, ill and sore. The first sign that I was beginning to lose the lining of my mouth was a sensation that my throat was starting to constrict. It felt frightening, as though the blockage would tighten until it stopped my windpipe and make me suffocate.

When my transplant manager did the 9am round that day, as usual he brought an entourage of junior doctors, trainees and foreign students with him. They examined me, discussed my case and debated whether my drug regime needed alteration, and then turned to leave.

'Excuse me,' I said to Simon, 'my throat has swelled up, and I'm worried that if it carries on I'm going to suffocate.'

'There's no way that will happen,' he reassured me, 'what you're feeling is quite normal and is the first sign of your membranes disintegrating. But don't worry, you'll continue to have a clear passage-way there.'

I didn't like the sensation at all.

Kath gave me a *Corsodyl* mouth-wash and told me in no uncertain terms it was the single most important thing I could do to aid my recovery. It is designed to make eating possible, and as I already knew, natural eating makes the difference between coming through or giving up. But the mouth-wash is truly disgusting. Every day my mouth became more sore, until the pain of it was unbearable. Imagine the very worst kind of mouth ulcer, on and under your tongue, inside your cheeks, and down your throat. Then double it. The pain makes eating impossibly painful.

Kath said, 'Use this mouth-wash six times a day if you can bear to, and every time you wake in the night, it will keep infection out while you have no immune system.'

Then I had a call from an acquaintance who had been through transplant and she said she couldn't stress in strong enough terms the importance of that mouth-wash. 'Just do it,' she said, it's more important than anything else.'

And I heard about a little boy whose mother felt that *Corsoldyl* had brought her son through transplant.

I took the advice on board, just as I always did, and through sobs and tears rinsed my mouth out and struggled on.

Now I couldn't chew, eat or swallow, and the nightmare began. Every single day Adrian dashed out to Ealing Broadway to find something to tempt me to eat through the pain. When he returned I looked at the food and said, 'I'm sorry Ade, I can't eat it.'

He never once got angry with me, but he did panic. Whenever I refused to eat he would say, 'Well you've got to eat something Fran, I'll see what I can do.' He would go into the little kitchen and prepare an alternative, and then he experimented with the hospital build-up drinks. I tried them but they were revolting.

Imagine it, I had lost my appetite completely, my taste buds were damaged, and my mouth had no lining. Putting any kind of food into my mouth was the last thing on earth I wanted to do. But even after my resolve to eat had gone, Adrian knew it would save my life. He had the patience of a saint, and when I couldn't swallow the drinks, he started to improve them by adding pureed banana. But the fruit acid made my mouth sear with pain, and made water stream from my eyes.

He tried everything and it broke my heart for him every time I failed to swallow, and I was angry with myself and disappointed that the pain was so much worse than I had predicted.

In the end I simply said, 'I'm sorry Ade, I can't drink these,' and he responded by getting a blender. He made me milk shakes and whizzed up my favourite foods, but I couldn't swallow anything. My weight was falling already, and we knew that unless I could eat, the alternative would be drip-feeding. Then my chance of coming out of hospital would be severely reduced, and I knew once my appetite had gone, it would be a bigger battle in the end.

One day when my eating was at its worst, I said to Adrian in a small voice, 'I think I could manage a little bit of macaroni cheese, or a crème caramel.'

'Yes!' he said, 'I'll be straight back.' He dashed to the supermarket and brought back a selection.

'I could just fancy a sloppy macaroni, and I think a caramel would be cooling for my throat.' I said to him.

Slowly but surely, I ate my way through a portion of each, taking tiny mouthfuls and weeping as I swallowed.

For the rest of my time in isolation that was my staple diet, and for several years afterwards I was unable to bear the thought of either. But nowadays macaroni cheese is the boys' favourite meal, and I find myself making it all the time.

Dear, dear Mum. Adrian told her what I was eating, and she asked for the Hammersmith booklet on food preparation for transplant patients. She started cooking home-made macaroni cheese for me, wearing plastic gloves as she worked, and adhering to every command in the booklet. Then she and Dad would drive to London with the chilled freshly cooked meal, and I ate it up, knowing every morsel was a sign of her love. She and Adrian were very, very strict with my food, they wouldn't take a single risk of giving me an infection because of their standards of kitchen hygiene.

As the days went by, my mouth and throat became worse. The twenty-four hour a day diamorphine being dispensed through my *Hickman line* made no improvement to my mouth. Before every meal the nurse gave me an extra surge of morphine to try to give me enough pain relief to allow me to eat, but it wore off very quickly.

They also gave me a cocaine mouth-wash to swill and spit out before every meal. At best it numbed the pain for a minute or two, but the effect wore off very quickly, and the numbing lessened every time I used it. But I battled on with my macaroni cheese and never lost the determination to carry on eating. I was fighting to prevent the day when a nurse would walk into my room with a drip to feed me. I knew that for me, it would have spelled the end.

Kath weighed me every morning and evening, and watched my weight loss like a hawk. Although the pounds were falling off, she felt I was just holding my own. After a few weeks I began to get the very first small cravings for food, just the tiniest signs of a new appetite. Sometimes it would be a sweet I fancied, which Adrian had to search for in double wrapped packaging. I wasn't allowed to eat anything in single packaging, so an ordinary Mars bar was out, but a packet of wrapped ones was allowed.

I could see the shadows caused by bright sunlight on the wall outside my window and knew it must be a hot summer. 'Phew it's boiling out there,' Adrian would say as he came back to me sucking a cool Solero ice-lolly. Suddenly I had a passion for an ice-cream too, and watched Adrian eating his with envy. But he didn't find any double-wrapped Soleros, so I never managed to have one of those.

One thing I certainly didn't fancy was a curry. Before transplant an Indian was my favourite food, and often Adrian came back to my room with a take-away. He became notorious as the one who made the entire ward stink, and he sat in front of me making the room smell awful. I plodded on with my macaroni cheese and a nurse would peep in and say 'Oh no, Ade is having his curry!'

Then I developed a fetish for fondant fancies, the little square iced cakes we used to eat at parties when I was a child. We checked with the nurses and they said I could eat some as long as they were double wrapped, or if I consumed the entire packet within six hours of opening it.

'I can't eat an entire box!' I said to Adrian.

'It doesn't matter, I'm going to find you some,' he said.

He came back with a box of six fondant fancies inside a cellophane packet, and we were given the all-clear.

'Right, start eating,' said Adrian, 'you've got to get through all these.'

After that, every time a nurse came into my room, I was discovered with my mouth round a pink, yellow or brown fondant fancy.

The things I missed most were fresh fruit, salad and vegetables, all of which were banned because of the risk of germs on the outside. Every meal had to be totally fresh and eaten on the day of purchase, and we must have wasted a lot of food in those weeks, but the important thing was, I carried on eating and my weight didn't drop low enough to keep me in hospital longer than necessary.

Chapter Fifteen

A Ray of Hope

ଔ ଯ ଓ ଯ

Somehow, Adrian managed to keep his spirits up, and even at my lowest times he was cheerful and encouraged other patients and the staff. The camaraderie helped him get through, and he was a pillar of strength for me.

He never moaned, and kept constantly busy, finding a video for me to watch, or a new, untouched magazine. I was only allowed a copy that had come from the back of the shelf, which was unlikely to have been handled. I wasn't well enough to watch a whole film, because I had absolutely no power of concentration, and even my two favourite films of all time, *Pretty Woman* and *Four Weddings and a Funeral*, couldn't hold my attention.

By now I had become too poorly to speak on the phone, although on a few occasions my guilt forced me to try, but I suffered dreadfully after talking.

I saved every ounce of my strength for the daily phone call from the boys, and never, ever failed to say a few words to them. Matthew told me what he had been learning with Kathryn the nanny, where Grandma had taken him in the car, and what Sebastian had done to annoy him. However bad things became, I always whispered to them, even when I was drifting in and out of consciousness from the pain relief. Then we said goodnight and I pictured the boys snuggled up under their duvets, and knew Grandma would give them the most special kiss from mummy in hospital.

My other highlight of each day was the arrival of post, a heap every single morning, people were so kind in keeping in touch with me. Adrian ripped open the envelopes and passed letters and cards to me, reading the words aloud when I was too ill to see them for myself. I had confided to a few friends that I felt stifled by the oppressiveness of my room, and longed for a real view from my window rather than the brick wall. In one morning's post, a packet arrived from a friend containing photographs of a tiny cottage in the country and its beautiful views. I could look at them and imagine myself there.

One message wasn't good news though. Adrian spent a lot of time on our computer sending emails to his IBM team, although he wasn't officially working.

One day I heard him say, 'Oh no! I don't believe it!'

'What's happened?'

'I've had an email from a woman at IBM saying Al Wenlock has been diagnosed with Hodgkinson's disease.'

This is a near relative of leukaemia and Al was one of my closest team colleagues at IBM. Four years earlier when I told Al about my diagnosis, he had been perched on the corner of my desk.

'How are things?' he had asked.

'Not brilliant actually. I've been diagnosed with leukaemia.'

As I said it, Al fainted and fell off the desk, crashing his head on the floor with a resounding thump. People flocked around us in the open-plan office and made him comfortable until he came round. As soon as he had been checked out in Casualty, we all collapsed in fits of giggles and the moment became entrenched in IBM folk-lore, as the day Al Wenlock fainted and fell off the desk. We smiled about it for weeks afterwards.

But now I recalled the incident with horror, it seemed so tragic and ironic that the man who reacted to my news with such instinctive shock, had been diagnosed with a similar condition. It was almost as if something inside him knew he would go the same way as me.

On my hospital pin-board were several lovely cards from Al and his wife, saying 'Keep going Fran, we're behind you,' and now he needed the same reassurance from me.

Since then Al has undergone chemotherapy and a bone marrow transplant, but isn't yet completely free of the disease. The news of his diagnosis was a terrible shock, and I realised sadly that leukaemia is far from rare.

Adrian spoke regularly on the phone to the Duchess of Kent who rang to ask for news of my progress. She made arrangements to visit me several times, especially during this period when I was seriously ill. Her immense concern extended to Adrian too, and she asked whether he would enjoy a visit to Queen's Club for a game of tennis with her coach. It would give Adrian a break, and use some of his pent-up energy. Because she knew he would worry about being away from me, Katherine suggested sitting with me herself for the entire afternoon he would be away.

When she arrived, I was feeling absolutely awful, and wasn't well enough to sit up or move. But the moment Katherine came into my room, she put me at ease and told me not to move on her account. She had no airs and graces, and told me she genuinely wanted to be there. This was so difficult to take in, but I was uplifted by her love and interest in me.

She spent the whole afternoon at my side, chatting and reading her favourite poems aloud. The drugs made me very sleepy and she told me not to worry a bit if I drifted off while she read. Then we shared many personal and private things and in the midst of my savage illness, a deep friendship and bond formed, that remains to this day.

Katherine combined concern with generosity, and never visited without bringing me a present. I began to tell her off and urge her not to buy things for me. She brought clothes, and when I scolded her for spending money she brought things from her own wardrobe, including an exquisite white nightie which became my favourite.

Now I have to make a confession, when Adrian was doing my laundry in the patient's washing room, he put the nightie in the same load as an orange tee shirt and it came out pale tangerine. He said nothing to me, knowing I would be gutted, and the nurses suggested he bought laundry bleach to soak the precious nightie in a bucket.

He was panicking about how to tell me the news, but eventually made the nightie white again, ironed and returned it to the cupboard. I was completely fooled, and he didn't tell me the truth until we came home, and I have the special gift to this day.

Each present Katherine brought was perfect and useful. During Wimbledon fortnight she brought a floppy hat from the shop and asked me to wear it instead of my baseball caps, because she thought it would be much prettier and more flattering. And she promised to take me out shopping to buy a wig when I was allowed out, as she knew I was obsessed with the state of my bald head. Before isolation I had bought a wig in a London store, and the Hammersmith had issued an NHS wig, but I was too embarrassed to wear either of them. I felt less conspicuous in a baseball cap.

One day she gave me a beautiful thick white Wimbledon bathrobe, and before I could reprimand her, she announced that it had been a gift from the Wimbledon shop whose staff had been moved on hearing my story and had sent best wishes for my recovery. Then she beamed and promised with absolute assurance that she would take me to Wimbledon the next year. She was totally confident I was going to make it, and her invitation was a huge tonic. I didn't expect it to come true, although I suspected she could arrange a ticket for me because of her connection to the club.

Sport was forced on me as a major feature of my recovery, as it was Adrian's diversion from my pain. He is utterly obsessed with Everton football club, and not long after my transplant was a historic FA cup final when Everton played against Liverpool. This was every birthday and Christmas present at once for Adrian, and he prepared for the match with gusto. Although I felt like death, he bought me an Everton shirt to wear in bed during the game, and he actually wrote to the club explaining about my transplant and asking for a signed photo for me. When it arrived he insisted on giving it pride of place on the wall. I drifted in and out of sleep during the game, and Adrian bounced around the room to watch his team win one-nil.

I remember 25th May very clearly. The Rugby World Cup was in full swing and Adrian was glued to our television for every game. One of the nurses was Australian, another a New Zealander, and during matches Adrian kept nipping down the corridor to tell them the latest scores. When England scored he ran down the ward hollering, and the nurses teased him and laughed. On 25th May, England were playing while the doctors were doing their round, and Simon Rule rushed into my room, straight past my bed and immersed himself in the current match with Adrian. I could hear them huffing and puffing about the England performance.

Another consultant, Jane Apperley, came into the room and spoke to me.

At first I couldn't take in what she was saying.

'We've got some potentially good news Fran. We've seen the very first signs of graft in your blood, and although it isn't showing up on the white cell blood count, we have looked at the blood on slides and have seen signs of graft taking place.'

'You mean my system is grafting on to the donor marrow?' I whispered in disbelief.

'Yes, we believe it is.'

This was the most incredible feeling. You never know, there can never be any certainty that a transplant will take. If it doesn't, you have a backup option of receiving your own blood and bone marrow back from storage, as my poor friend Jenny Hamilton had done, but that only takes you back to square one.

I was over the moon, 'Oi you two,' I rasped as energetically as I could, 'stop watching the telly and listen to my amazing news.'

Adrian turned to listen to the consultant and Simon Rule butted in, 'Oh yes, I was about to tell you!'

Adrian was as excited and overwhelmed as me, even though the progress was tiny, we knew it should herald the production of new white blood cells, and begin to give me an immune system.

Adrian got straight on the phone to our parents, and our hopes began to rise.

For the next few days there was a tiny white cell count in my blood, which Adrian marked on his charts, and we dared to believe I might pull through.

Two days later, on Day Fifteen, we celebrated our sixth wedding anniversary in my room. I had managed to order a Tweetie Pie golf club cover by phone for Adrian to remind him of baby Sebastian who we all thought looked just like the cartoon bird. Adrian was very moved by my efforts for him, it was the first thing I had been able to do for myself for ages. We had a lot of cards for that anniversary, and despite the circumstances, I have happy memories of it as a major milestone.

At that stage Simon Rule left the Hammersmith for a new post in Exeter as a consultant. We were sorry to see him go, and Adrian decided to make his last visit a memorable one. Simon had always been fascinated by my refusal to show my bald head and used to ask, 'Do you sleep in that baseball cap Fran?'

'Yes, I'm never taking it off.'

Just before Simon's last round at nine am, Adrian stuck a note on the top of my head with a piece of sticky-tack and then covered it with my cap.

After Simon had finished examining me, Adrian said, 'We both wish you luck and all the best,' and I lifted my baseball cap.

Simon looked stupefied, and then burst out laughing as he read the words on my head, 'Bye bye Simon!' His entourage of junior doctors burst into giggles and even I laughed.

Just before he left I said, 'If I get through this Simon, I'll owe you so much, we promise to come and find you and take you out to lunch to thank you.'

His laugh turned to a sad smile.

Chapter Sixteen

Fighting for my Life

ଓ ଯ ଓ ଯ

To our delight, my white cell count continued its gradual rise. By Day Twenty-two it was 0.26, and then it rose each day to 0.38, 0.4 and 0.6. We could see we were very close to the magic number 1.0 that signals a genuine development of immunity. But you never know whether it will begin to fall again, and we prayed for the small but steady increase to continue.

Suddenly, on 8th June, Day Twenty-seven since transplant, my white cell count leapt to 1.05. It was my father's birthday. Adrian was ecstatic and tried to phone our parents to tell them the wonderful news. He tracked all four of them down at our own house, while they were cleaning the place from top to bottom, in anticipation of me being allowed home from hospital. Working to instructions from the Hammersmith, they were having the house de-fumigated, shampooing the carpets and three-piece suite, and going over the inside from top to toe.

As I lay listening to Adrian praising their hard work, I felt that my house must have been the dirtiest in Britain. But it was vital to eliminate any germs and minimise the risk of me picking up infection at home.

'Listen,' Adrian said to my father, who I pictured standing in our hall in his scruffy work clothes, 'we've got some fabulous news,' and he passed the phone to me.

'Dad, my white cell count has gone up to 1.05,' I whispered.

'Oh darling, that's the best birthday present I could possibly have,' he said, and I tried not to weep.

I began to hope it wouldn't be long before I was allowed out of hospital.

But the very next day I began to feel violently sick. Before Adrian went out for the daily food shopping, he had spoken to the nurses and suggested keeping me on my existing anti-sickness drugs, and adding an additional one if I didn't improve. As usual, he was acting as an unofficial consultant on the case, it amused me the way the staff took note of his advice.

But while Adrian was out, I started to suffer the most terrible pains in my stomach. I was terrified and started to vomit with the searing, ripping pain. The nurses were wonderful, and brought heat packs to wrap around my body to help reduce the cramp. In the midst of the panic, a nurse popped her head around my door and said, 'Fran you've got a visitor.'

At my own request, I never had visitors in isolation, except the Duchess, my parents, my brother Nick or the children.

'Please tell them to leave,' I begged, I'm too ill to see them.'

'It's Lloyd Scott from Anthony Nolan,' she replied.

I knew Lloyd quite well. He was a fireman who had a transplant several years before me and was my mother's idol. She had first heard about him from a cover story of the Anthony Nolan magazine, when Lloyd ran the London marathon with his donor after transplant. His recovery had been amazing, and in the photo he had looked fitter and healthier than his donor! Lloyd inspired my mother and she set her sights on my recovery mirroring his own. She called him Fireman Sam, and used to say to me, 'if Fireman Sam can do it, you can do it Fran, he's my hero.' After his recovery he got a job with Anthony Nolan.

But I couldn't face seeing anyone so I said, 'Tell him I'm too ill.'

A few moments later the nurse returned, 'He's insistent on seeing you, he has something from your donor.'

Lloyd wouldn't take no for an answer, and bounded down the corridor into my room, saying, 'I've got something amazing for you, and I know you'll want to have it.'

I hadn't enough energy to argue any more.

'We've just received this card and present for you at Anthony Nolan,' he said enthusiastically, 'and I came straight here because I knew it would mean so much to you.'

I asked him to open the card because I wasn't strong enough.

There was a lovely message from my donor, 'Dear friend, just hoping you're doing OK and I'm thinking of you,' and because she wasn't allowed to sign her name, she had drawn a smiley face instead. It was to become her shorthand signature.

The gift was a beautiful china ornament. I had hoped and longed to hear from her, but it seemed so generous when she had already given her bone marrow to save my life.

But I was glad Lloyd visited me, because he gave me a tip that may have helped me recover, he explained the importance of visualising my leukaemia being defeated inside me. 'Imagine a mental image of your mutant cells being defeated by the new marrow,' he said. 'Any image, whatever works for you – then spend time every single day visualising it killing the leukaemia inside.'

I began to picture my mutant cells being eaten by little *pac-men* inside my body. I spent hours lying in silence, visualising the process of defeat, and I'm grateful for Lloyd's advice which I have heard has helped others with cancer.

The only other visitor during my isolation was Tony Morland, Chief Executive of Anthony Nolan who brought me beautiful flowers and a new baseball cap to add to my collection. I was profoundly touched by his kindness in thinking of me.

I continued to be very ill indeed, and on one of my worst days, the nurses had an unexpected visit from the Duchess of Kent's driver. On the previous evening, Katherine had attended a concert by José Carreras, and she discovered he had undergone a bone marrow transplant for leukaemia a few years earlier. Backstage after the performance, she told him about me and asked whether he could give me encouragement, so he had signed her programme and written in huge scrawl, 'You can do it Fran – from Carreras.'

Katherine phoned to check I had received it, and was so excited to have met someone who had survived the trauma and could give me hope. Her excitement was infectious and encouraging. I felt and still feel, that I'm insignificant, and it's impossible to explain how good it is to be cared for by a person who is important. I know the Duchess wouldn't see it this way, but I'm in awe of her, and her support was one of the key factors that gave me the will to fight and pull through. I recall one of our first conversations when Katherine said to me, 'Please don't treat me as a Royal, I'm just a normal person like you, the only difference is I'm from Yorkshire, you're from Warwick. First and foremost you're my friend.'

Katherine is very unassuming about her influence, but she made all the difference in the world for me, and in part, I owe my recovery to her.

By now the staff were confident I had enough immunity to allow my first short trip out, as long as I met only my parents and children who had been in isolation at their house. As a trial run, on 10th June, I attempted my first trip outside my room. Adrian helped me to my feet and led me out of the Dacie Ward along the ground floor corridor and out of the hospital building. It felt dangerous and terrifying to be out of isolation.

Behind the Hammersmith is Wormwood Scrubs prison, with a little piece of wasteland and open field lying between the sites. I tried to walk for a while, but very quickly said to Adrian, 'I can't go any further.'

He helped me to a wooden bench overlooking the prison, and I sat down in a heap feeling absolutely lousy, 'I'm not going to be able to walk back,' I said. The total distance from my room couldn't have been more than seventy-five yards, but it was too far. My limbs and head and my very bones ached with tiredness and I felt so cold, despite wearing a thermal bobble hat in June. The weakness can't be described. And the air seemed so dirty and polluted, I was convinced the atmosphere was loaded with germs and I tried to take only shallow short breaths.

'You'll make it back, and if you can't, I'll carry you,' Adrian said.

It took every ounce of my determination to lean on him and creep back to the ward. The journey took a long time and I realised our walk had been far too ambitious. That adventure really frightened me.

The walk had been an experiment to assess my readiness for going home, but all that had been proved by it was my fear of infection and utter, all-consuming weakness.

As soon as we returned, the nurses interrogated us and made notes on our experience. They wanted to know how we felt, and whether we were ready for the responsibility of managing my drug regime away from the hospital.

Only a few days later, on 13th June, the Hammersmith discharged me. I can remember feeling disbelief combined with fear, against a background of excitement, because things had moved on very quickly. As soon as the doctor told me I was free to go, I wanted to leave immediately, afraid he may change his mind.

Within a couple of hours Adrian packed away every item from my room. I lay on the bed, exhausted, and watched as he unpinned literally hundreds of cards from my walls, packed up the computer, clothes and post. I only managed to leaf through the piles of medical articles and information I had collected and decided what needed to go home.

Although I hadn't moved from my bed, I was mentally and physically drained, but determined to say goodbye to Professor Goldman. So, while Adrian carried boxes to the car park, I made my first solo journey. I walked very, very slowly along the corridor to the secretary's room, anxious to thank her for her kindness. Karen had been remarkably good to us, before and during transplant, and had often rung and popped along to say hello.

I wasn't able to walk properly, it was more of a stagger, and when I arrived in Karen's office she could see I was about to collapse.

'Fran, sit down, sit down,' she urged and I flopped into her chair. Unfortunately, Professor Goldman wasn't in his room and I would have to walk back to the ward. I thanked Karen but wasn't able to say another word, all that was in my mind was an overwhelming certainty that I wouldn't make it back. I have honestly never felt so ill in my life as I did at that time.

The situation struck me as highly ironic, I was being discharged because things were apparently going so well, but I felt more sick than at any time during transplant. I felt utterly weak, the best way to describe it is a china doll made of fragile bone-china who would break at the slightest touch.

I did make it to Room One and collapsed in the chair, aware of Adrian sorting out the last few boxes while he waited for my drug packs to arrive so we could set off for Warwick.

Suddenly Professor Goldman came into the room to say goodbye, and I was profoundly touched. But it meant I had to get out of the chair and I didn't know whether my legs would support me. We had bought a bottle of champagne and a Tigger tie as a thank-you gift for him and I lifted them while Adrian took a photo. I remember thinking I was going to drop the bottle because it felt so heavy in my hand.

Everything swooned and wobbled and I thought I would fall.

Professor Goldman said, 'You've got to be so careful Fran, you're not through the woods by any means, but it's time to try going home. You can always come back if it doesn't work out.'

I knew I would be at the Hammersmith twice a week anyway, and my first appointment was only two days ahead, but it was a major milestone and I felt a surge of gratitude to the Professor.

All the nurses came to say goodbye, and Adrian thanked them sincerely. The room was now as bare and empty as the day I arrived, and I looked at it bleakly. Unlike that first day, I hadn't an ounce of energy for speeches or emotion. I turned to Adrian and said, 'I'm not going to be able to make it to the car, I'm sorry.'

The hospital gave him permission to bring the car to the nearest doorway and he supported my weight and lifted me inside.

Deep down I felt a little voice saying 'This is it, you're going home!' but I couldn't feel happy. Although Adrian had cleaned the car interior from top to bottom, I was paranoid about dirt, and we drove home with all the air vents and windows closed. I had the beginning of an immune system, but knew I mustn't be exposed to any germs. I was convinced the air was heavy with bacteria of every kind, and an obsession with cleanliness developed from that day. I wouldn't touch anything inside the car.

After six weeks cooped up in a small room, being in the car was a frightening experience. Everything felt out of control, and other vehicles seemed so big and fast and much too close. I kept telling Adrian to slow down, my mind couldn't cope with the pace of normal life any more. But when we pulled off the motorway into my parents' village, the countryside seemed more beautiful to me than I had ever seen it. Spring had matured into the fullness of summer while I had been shut away, and it seemed even lovelier than I remembered.

We drove into my parents' drive and I was exhausted, unsure why I felt so bad, because I hadn't done anything, except lie in bed full of drugs and tubes for weeks, but my energy levels hadn't been tested. I wasn't able to enjoy the family welcome, and showed no excitement or emotion, and my parents could see I was about to fall. I wanted to hug and thank Kathryn the nanny for all she had done, but couldn't manage a word. Adrian helped me into an armchair and I collapsed into it. That was when I first had the sensation of being breakable, hating to be touched, in case I was damaged. Kathryn took the boys out of the room because I couldn't cope with their effusiveness and I sat in silence.

It was a very strange experience, I wanted to be home, and was pleased to be there, but also full of fear. As I sat in stillness, the thought dawned on me that I may not make it. However bad things had been until that point, I had always managed to speak, but now for the first time I had no resources. I wondered if my old self was lost forever, and whether I would ever regain my confidence. More had been killed in that radiation than my immune system, my bubbly personality had died too. I thought I would never feel strong again, or be able to stand up for myself.

Our first visit was short, because I was craving my own bed after such a long day, so we said goodbye and drove to our own home. I hadn't seen it for weeks, and our road looked utterly beautiful to me, with its drapery of chestnut trees in the full leaf of high summer. In my precarious situation, I was appreciating life more than ever, and felt very, very sad. We had planned to leave the boys with my parents until I was well enough to be with them, and I knew recovery would be both long and difficult.

I gathered every last ounce of will and shuffled indoors. Home felt so clean and safe, like a cocoon, my own personal isolation unit, where even the dogs and the boys hadn't walked with muddy feet. For the first time that day I felt happy, as I stumbled up the stairs and into our bedroom which looked so very pretty after the Hammersmith. I have never felt so thankful as that moment when I crawled under our own duvet. I can only describe it as all of the best home-comings rolled into one, almost as if I had found myself in heaven.

As the days passed I settled into a very quiet routine. Adrian nursed me at home and I continued to eat and rest and try to build up a little strength. Most days he drove me to my parents' home to spend an hour with the boys, but I found even that very tiring. The weather was lovely, and as I wasn't allowed any sun on my skin for a year after radiation treatment, I would sit in the shade and watch Matthew and Sebastian play.

But I wasn't well enough to chat, even with the children, and Mum fielded their questions for me. It sounds awful that I hadn't got the energy to speak to people, but that's the way it was. I had nothing inside me, no strength for communication or emotion.

I was delighted to see the strong bond that had formed between Kathryn and the boys, they really liked her, and she kept them very busy. When she could tell I was worse than usual, after a few minutes she would take them out to the park to give me a rest. I didn't fear losing their love, and honestly hadn't even the smallest resources for joining in.

A couple of days after I came home, Dee asked if she could visit. She had been so faithful in her contact at hospital, ringing Adrian daily to update him on life at home. We agreed she could call, and Adrian met her in the hall with a plastic hospital apron for her to wear. She was so afraid of passing on germs to me and washed her hands in iodine, then came into the lounge, and sat at the furthest edge of the room from me and we just looked at each other. I felt like a little breakable doll, and just like one, I couldn't smile or speak. But it was such a precious moment seeing her again, one of my dearest friends who had stood by me through thick and thin. I had been very afraid that I would lose my friends because of the treatment, and the isolation which would take me away from normal contact.

But Dee was obviously still the same, chatting about her children Jade and Kurtis and what was happening in ordinary life in the real world. She hid her shock at the change in me, and later said that even then she had seen a glimmer of the old Fran. Adrian never left my side, and I tried to look and feel normal, but couldn't. It wasn't me inside my body any more, it felt as though I were outside looking in. While she chatted I thought 'You're not yourself Fran, and you can never be the natural, giggly you again.'

I was to feel that way for many months to come, and preferred to be alone without reminders of what used to be.

The Hammersmith had given us detailed rules and regulations for my recuperation at home. I read them avidly and took every aspect to heart, absolutely determined that if the transplant had succeeded, I would maximise my chances of getting well. I knew that many transplant patients die from infections caught during recovery, and I was desperate to avoid that. But I felt so very ill, and couldn't see how I was going to make it.

With a very poor immune system even a common cold can be fatal, and as immunity is so low, any virus gets a hold very quickly. The Hammersmith had given us a procedure for this danger, and if I caught any illness, I must go to the nearest hospital and take intravenous antibiotics without delay. We were instructed to take my temperature on waking and last thing every night, as this gives the best early indicator of presence of infection, and if it rose to 37.5 degrees, I must phone the Dacie Ward. There was particular concern about me because I lived at two hours driving distance from London.

Just a couple of weeks after my discharge, at bed-time my temperature read 37.5. We phoned the Hammersmith and they asked me to take a reading every hour and report it by phone. By midnight it had risen to 38 degrees, the level requiring hospitalisation.

'Drop everything and get to Warwick Hospital,' Dacie Ward told me. I was afraid, and wanted to go to the

Hammersmith because I trusted them as the centre of competence for my case and drug regime. But I had no choice, and Adrian drove me into Warwick.

The Hammersmith liaised with the hospital by phone and arranged for me to have a single room in the Haematology ward where I could be placed in relative isolation. But as it was late at night, my haematologist was off duty, and I had to wait for the duty doctor to finish her rounds in casualty and make her way to see me a couple of hours later.

When she finally arrived, she gave me a thorough examination. I lay there wondering why she didn't put me straight on to antibiotics, as the Hammersmith had recommended.

'I think we need to leave it to the morning and speak to the Hammersmith,' she said.

I turned to Adrian, 'If they aren't going to do anything tonight I don't want to stay here. I'm so frightened, and I keep thinking of all the germs in the hospital, even though it looks clean in here, I know it can't be.'

Adrian rang for the nurse. 'I'm going to drive Fran home now and take her to the Hammersmith in the morning.'

'You can't possibly do that, we can't allow you to discharge yourself!' she said.

'Then I'll have another opinion.'

Eventually a second doctor came to examine me and Adrian explained our problem and my concern. He seemed more reasonable, 'Look I totally understand your logic, but I advise you to stay here where we can monitor you Fran. However, if you're adamant to discharge yourself, then I won't stop you.'

So I left, and first thing next morning Adrian drove me to the Hammersmith where I waited in the out-patients clinic to see a specialist. My temperature was still high but I never thought the hospital would keep me in, expecting simply to be given drugs and discharged. As we waited, I tried to keep my eyes on the floor and escape anybody's notice. Throughout the last two years I had sat in this very room looking at patients like me after their transplant and knew how I appeared to other people – sick, wasted, looking as though there was no hope of a future. Now I felt no desire for the camaraderie of previous visits when I had chatted happily to other patients and made friends. I wouldn't be pleased to see anyone, nor for them to look at me in this dreadful state.

As soon as I had been examined they re-admitted me, and my heart sank. I knew it was probably for the best, but felt I had made no progress at all, and knew this kind of infection spelled the end for many leukaemia patients after transplant. I begged to be put back on Dacie Ward which felt like a second home, and where I trusted the staff implicitly, but there were no beds. They put me on a ward high above the ground floor Dacie Ward, and I hated it, hated everything about it. The July sun beat down through the windows and made the room completely oppressive. I sat like a statue waiting for Adrian to drive to Warwick and back to fetch our overnight bags, and didn't know what was going to happen to me.

I was looked after by Simon Rule's replacement, Jonathon Blackwell, and I remember watching Jonathon and Professor Goldman at the foot of my bed discussing my fever, and nobody could work out what was wrong. I felt so afraid, fearing this simple infection after coming through all the struggles of a transplant.

'I think she's got an infection in her *Hickman line*,' Jonathon was saying to Professor Goldman, 'and the only way we can be sure is by taking the line out.'

My *Hickman line* had been left in my chest as a last resort so all drugs could be dispensed through it, which was preferable to having multiple injections in the early stages after transplant. Now they administered antibiotics through it to try to bring my infection down.

A chest x-ray showed a patch of shading near the lung, but it was inconclusive, and I had a painful endoscopy which found nothing significant. The hospital carried out several other fruitless tests, and with my birthday only days away, I begged to be allowed home on the Sunday to celebrate with the boys.

The Hammersmith agreed, and then I continued to pester and pressurise for discharge, because my parents ruby wedding anniversary was only a week later. I think the hospital suspected I was making excuses, and the staff were not keen to allow me out. I felt very depressed, and aware that my illness had put the lives of everyone I loved into disarray.

In the middle of it all, Adrian was taken seriously ill too. He became suddenly sick and dizzy and everyone was worried he would have to leave me in case he passed on an infection. My ward had no access to a suitable doctor so Adrian went to the casualty department and waited ten hours until midnight to see a doctor. It turned out he had a middle ear infection that could be cleared up by antibiotics and was no danger to me, so we were allowed to stay together after all.

During one of our walks to the scrub-land behind the Hammersmith, I received an unexpected gift. The weather was absolutely scorching that summer, and the Duchess of Kent had been worried about me suffering in hospital. When I returned to my room, I discovered on my bed an exquisite slim thermos flask, with a beautiful little cup for a lid. Katherine said she thought it would be useful for me to keep cool drinks in. Just as ever, she had done exactly the right thing to lift my spirits.

I had been back in hospital for two weeks, and just before the weekend of my parents' anniversary, Jonathon Blackwell suddenly charged into my room. 'I've got the go ahead – we're taking your *Hickman line* out!'

'Crikey – how?' I asked, feeling a sense of panic. The line had been a part of me for so long that I felt afraid to be without it.

'We'll simply pull it out, as soon as I can get the things I need.'

'Do I need an anaesthetic?'

'No, but I'll give you a tablet which will ensure you have no memory of the procedure afterwards.'

I glanced at the clock. 'Look, it's *Coronation Street* at half-past seven and that's my number one priority when I'm in hospital. Will you be finished by then, and will I be compus mentis for watching it?'

Jonathon laughed and said, 'Yeah, yeah, you'll be fine.'

So he gave me the tablet, and I don't remember a thing about what happened next. Later Jonathon joked that he had put a foot on my chest and had a right tug of war to get the line out, although Adrian said it took no more than a couple of yanks to remove. The first thing I remember is sitting up in bed watching Corrie Street. I always had several nursing checks in that half hour, and we teased the nurses because we knew they chose to look after me during their favourite programme.

But the next morning I couldn't remember a single thing that had happened during the episode, and Adrian had to talk me through the entire programme. It was weird.

But Jonathon had been right, as soon as my *Hickman line* was removed, my temperature started to drop, and within twenty-four hours I was normal and discharged from the hospital.

'I told you so, we should have done that ages ago!' Jonathon quipped.

Chapter Seventeen

Meeting my Deadline

ରୁ ଯ ଓ ଯ

The rest of the summer was a time for recuperation at home while my parents continued to look after the boys. I saw them every day, and went through good times and bad.

In August we celebrated Matthew's third birthday in our garden with Dee and her family. I felt quite strong that day, my blood count had climbed again to a respectable level, and I sat in the shade a little apart from the others for safety. As I sat watching the fun I had a sudden and totally new feeling. I wasn't normal by any means, but had the first faint sensation that I was enjoying myself. It was like the beginning of a flame, only a flicker, but an encouragement that some day in future, I might become me.

Dee was insistent that she wanted to try out the kids' water-slide into the paddling pool, and in a moment of madness she persuaded me to join her. We made holes for our legs in two black bin liners to wear like nappies while we slid into the water. Adrian and my parents looked shocked at the change in me, and I knew I had reached a major turning point.

After the visitors had left, little Matthew pedalled up to me on his plastic tractor. He clambered off and said, 'Look in my trailer mummy, there's something for you.'

I reached down, expecting one of his usual offerings – an interesting stone or a scribbly picture. But I saw a tiny box in his trailer. 'What the heck is that?' I asked.

Adrian said softly, 'Have a look.'

Inside the box I found the most beautiful sapphire ring, bluer than any stone I've ever seen. Immediately I burst into tears and hugged Adrian, 'Why have you done this?'

Matthew was running about in the sheer excitement of the moment, and I kept weeping, 'Why Adrian? You've supported me through all this, so I should be giving *you* a present. I can't believe you've done this.'

And he just hugged me.

I checked in at the Hammersmith every fortnight for tests, and steadily my immune system continued to grow. But I had one huge barrier to regaining any inner peace. Every three months the hospital carried out a Polymeraise Chain Reaction test, PCR, which is the finest level of detection known for leukaemia. At every test, residual leukaemia was still detected in me; the level fluctuated and was never constant, but always there. Despite everything I had been through, the transplant didn't seem to have killed off all of the mutant cells.

Katie was another patient who was an amazing source of inspiration to me at this time. She had been through her transplant and was about to get married, and she was ahead of me in her recovery. One day we bumped into each other in out-patients at our check-up, and she told me she was having flying lessons.

'You're amazing,' I said. 'How did you get your life back together again?'

'You will too Fran, you will. It's a very slow process and you have to be patient, but it comes. Gradually you'll get your energy back.'

Katie was such an encouragement, but only a year later she lost her own battle. Her death was another distressing proof that you're not out of the woods for a very long time with leukaemia.

Since my transplant I had never made an effort to look nice, always wearing a baseball cap, tee shirt and jeans and sitting still and silent. During a hospital visit that summer, the nursing sister took me on one side. 'Come on Fran, it's time you made an effort now. Try wearing a bit of make-up, or jewellery to spruce yourself up, it'll make you feel so much better. You've got some hair growing back and it would do you good to feel smart.'

'It doesn't seem worth it, I only sit at home or come here for a check-up.' But I knew she was right, although it was to be many more weeks before I took any notice.

My hair was the biggest problem. One of the post-transplant drugs had made my hair grow back in tight black corkscrews, utterly different to my straight fair hair of the past. I hated it and no amount of brushing stopped the tight black curls sticking flat to my scalp. The nurses encouraged me by promising my old hair would come back when the drugs were out of my system.

But I had one big incentive to improve my appearance. Matthew was due to begin nursery school in September 1995 and I was really keen to meet the target instead of delaying it.

We moved the boys home again, in preparation for Matthew's big day, the occasion which was even more momentous for me than him. Throughout my treatment the press had predicted that I wouldn't live to see my child's first day at school, and I was absolutely determined to prove them wrong. That autumn I looked as though I was at death's door, but I planned to take Matthew myself and hide under my baseball cap, hoping no-one would speak to me. Thankfully no parents knew my situation and the school had been wonderful about it.

So we dressed Matthew in his tiny new uniform and Adrian took us to school. I kept my head down all the time that I was out of the car. That first day must have been a nightmare for Matthew who had been in isolation for months on end and was suddenly faced with a room full of twenty toddlers charging about. He was mesmerised and stood close to me and wouldn't let me leave. His wonderful teacher, Mrs Henderson reassured me he would be fine, and I held myself together for his sake, even though I felt like sobbing.

As we drove home, I acknowledged in my secret heart that I had passed the deadline I'd feared more than any other. The words written in the press had gnawed away at my confidence, but I had made it and lived to see Matthew's first day at school.

Later on his teacher told me she was concerned about Matthew as he never, ever spoke. In fact he didn't open his mouth once during his first term, although Mrs Henderson told me not to worry and that it was hardly surprising after all he had been through. During the second term he did begin to speak to other children, and I'll never forget the day she rushed out at the end of school and said, 'He has spoken to me!' I have wondered about his quietness so much, Matthew is a naturally shy child, and quieter than his younger brother, but I also believe my transplant happened at a critical stage of his development. He was old enough to understand and feel the pain of separation from me, and also to miss the company of other children during isolation.

But even after starting nursery, poor little Matthew couldn't be a normal child, because every time there was a case of chicken-pox at school, I had to collect him at once and keep him at home. I then had to drive to Warwick Hospital for an emergency booster of *Zovirax* cells to help my immune system to fight off what can be a killer virus post-transplant.

Chapter Eighteen

Nick

ෆ ෨ ඐ ෨

When I first set out to write this book, I never suspected it would include this chapter. But throughout the time it has taken to write my story, my only brother Nick has fought a battle of his own. I decided to go ahead with the book despite the trauma we have experienced as a family, losing Nick to a cancerous brain tumour in January 2001.

My story would not be complete without this section, which I have written as a tribute to Nick, who was both brother and friend.

Although he never knew it, my brother was one of the main reasons I had fought so hard to have a family of my own with Adrian. While I was still a child myself, I decided to have two children, and mirror my own upbringing that seemed completely perfect.

I was so thankful for my elder brother, the play-mate who grew up to become my friend, and whose social circle was mine. Although I was always the little sister, for some reason I had been accepted and included by his mates who were three years older than me.

Nick and I had always been extremely close. I looked up to him, respecting him for the self-confidence I lacked, but teasing him mercilessly. As we grew older I began to confide in him, and we were always there for each other, unlike many of my friends who seemed to have nothing in common with their siblings.

Our childhood summer holidays were particularly special. From an early age, our parents took us on an annual package holiday to the Mediterranean – still the happiest memories of my brother. Dad would build us a speed-boat out of sand, and we ate picnics on the quietest beach we could find. I can still see one picnic in my mind's eye, Nick throwing his hard boiled egg up into the air like a ball, showing off and making us laugh, then tripping and falling backwards into the sea. I don't know if he found the egg.

I walked to meet him after school every day, and we would squabble all the way home. When Mum called us indoors for supper we were allowed to eat in the lounge on trays. Both Nick and I would race for the favourite armchair with the best view of the television. One day I determined to reach the chair first, so I plonked my supper tray on the seat to claim it, and then not to be out-done, Nick lunged backwards and sat on my meal. We laughed and fought like the best of brothers and sisters. Which is what we were. How I miss him now.

But the incident I want to record is the remarkable coincidence of Nick's life that occurred in the autumn after my transplant. Although during the early stages of my treatment, Nick had proved to be a mis-match as a bone marrow donor for me, he remained committed to the process of helping Anthony Nolan fight against leukaemia. He had taken part in the IBM bike ride and remained on the donor register in the hope that he could help to save someone else's life. Although the chance of being selected as a donor is very slim – only about 1 % of donors on the register will be used in transplant – Nick was chosen in 1995, the year of my own transplant. While I was still in the Hammersmith, Nick began telling me that he'd been contacted by Anthony Nolan as a potential donor, and he went through the various stages of blood tests to confirm the possible match. By the time I was recuperating at home it sounded very likely that

Nick would be used, and in October he was booked into the London clinic to have his bone marrow harvested.

In the most unlikely of scenarios, after one of my weekly check-ups at the Hammersmith, Adrian took me (in baseball cap) to visit my brother who had just donated his own marrow to a stranger. For once I sat on his bed, and was the visitor not the patient.

At the time Nick sent an anonymous note to the recipient, and much later he discovered his bone marrow had gone to a boy in Denmark, and only six months before Nick lost his life, he finally had a letter from the young boy telling his own story. He had suffered a great deal with emotional problems in addition to the medical traumas, but Nick's bone marrow had saved his life. By the time he received the letter, Nick was very ill, but hearing from the recipient put him on a huge high. It was a lovely moment during the saddest of times for our family, and Nick, his wife, and my parents all felt the thrill of him saving a life.

In the depths of sadness that I have experienced since losing my brother, I've thought long and hard about the strangeness of our lives. Our futures hang by gossamer threads, and can break in an instant. I had a fight and won, but my brother's battle was tougher. His death has left all of us with unanswerable questions that have rocked our faith and our world to its foundations.

But the bottom line is this, I loved Nick with an intensity carved even deeper by his death, my brother who in bravery and character, was a giant of a man.

Chapter Nineteen

Anne

 CR ED CR ED

In November Adrian returned to work full-time at IBM, and our family life began to assume a more normal pattern. Kathryn continued to work for us as nanny while I recovered, and I couldn't have managed without her in the early months. She remains a very dear friend to me and is often in touch with the boys.

The next few weeks were difficult, as many of the leukaemia patients I had come to know either deteriorated or lost their fight to live. All too often the Hammersmith would tell me I had lost another friend. During my grieving, my supporters tried to introduce me to people they knew with success stories, and one of these was Chris Corbin, the London restaurant-owner who has done so much to raise awareness for the cause since his own transplant. Even though he is a tremendously busy man, he visited me during one of my blood transfusions at the Hammersmith, looking the picture of health just a year after his transplant. That visit began to change my outlook on my own future.

I continued to receive numerous letters from my donor, her name always whited out by Anthony Nolan, and I slowly learned a little more about her. She wrote huge long newsy letters in reply to my painfully executed scrawly notes, and I was thrilled every time I heard from her. My hands still shook so much I could barely sign my name.

Anthony Nolan said they would honour their promise that we could meet a year after transplant, and I didn't know that as often as I had pestered Marjorie Gordon-Box, my donor had done the same. We were desperate to meet each other, and a year after my treatment, Marjorie finally gave me a name and phone number. Anne, at last I knew she was Anne.

But after all the anticipation, I was too nervous to ring, and decided I'd write to the address in Liverpool. Adrian had only one concern – 'Does she support Liverpool or Everton? – you must find out Fran.' We suggested a first meeting on June 19th at the Anthony Nolan premises in London where Marjorie would introduce us to each other.

As so often in my story, timing turns out to be all-important. The day after I had been given my donor's name, I attended the opening of new laboratories at the Hammersmith. The Duchess of Kent was conducting the official ceremony and it was my first day out, a year after transplant. I had a little bit of short hair, but no confidence yet, and it terrified me to be in a crowd as I still feared germs, but I was longing to meet Katherine again.

As soon as we arrived I was approached by the Chief Executive of Anthony Nolan who said the Duchess was anxious to see me. She was deep in conversation with someone else and I expected to wait my turn, but as soon as she saw me, Katherine flung her arms out and shouted, 'My dear Fran, how lovely to see you!' She hugged me like a true friend and I felt totally special and loved.

'Have you got any photos of the boys?' she asked, and eagerly looked at snaps from my bag. 'How they've grown since the pictures of them on my bedroom wall!'

But unbeknown to us, a photographer caught every moment of our meeting on film, and later sold the pictures to *Hello!* magazine. I had no idea we had been photographed until a friend rang to say she had seen me in the magazine, and I feared Katherine would think I had given permission, but as usual, I hadn't even been consulted. The camera lens was so efficient you can even make out my sons' faces in the pictures.

An even more dramatic outcome of the launch happened as a result of meeting Professor Goldman. 'Hello, how are you?' he hailed me, then getting straight down to business, 'you know we've been detecting residual leukaemia ever since your transplant. The figure has been pretty low, but in this last result it has shot up and I feel we've got to take some action. When you come down next week we'll sort out what we're going to do.'

'What can you do?' I panicked.

'Possibly ask your original donor to donate some white cells and blast your body with them, to see if your immune system will gee up and start fighting. Or consider a second transplant. You haven't had any serious Graft versus Host symptoms, and in a way that's a pity, because a limited rejection actually encourages your system to fight. We'll talk next week.'

Then he moved on, circulating with the other guests and I stood, glass in hand, feeling absolutely gutted, as though the breath had gone out of me. This eventuality had never crossed my mind. I had been to hell and back for a transplant, but it appeared I still had leukaemia, and it was coming back with a vengeance. Standing amidst the hum of social conversation and polite laughter, I faced the reality that I may have to undergo a second transplant to get rid of the disease, knowing that the chances of success a second time are far lower than the first. All the patients I knew well had reached a count of zero after transplant, Chris Corbin, and Lloyd Scott who my Mum called Fireman Sam. Neither of them ever had a positive reading after reaching zero, and I felt so jealous.

The Duchess had left and I couldn't see Adrian anywhere. I searched the room blindly and at last caught sight of him, but could hardly get my words out. 'Take me home, Ade, I have to get out of here.'

I remember the journey home with my parents being a nightmare. No-one spoke and I felt as though the bottom had fallen out of my world.

That night Adrian encouraged me to be positive, and I shouted, 'No Ade, not this time, you have to let me feel sorry for myself now. I've had a bloody transplant but I've still got leukaemia, and right now I can't see the point in any of it.'

I needed space and time to take in the news I had never anticipated. As I looked back on that first year I knew the warning signs had been there all along but I had blotted them out, and I had been stupid to do it.

The news had another dreadful implication for me – I knew Anthony Nolan wouldn't sanction a meeting with my donor if we had to undergo further treatment. All my hopes had been focussed on June 19th and the joy of meeting Anne at last.

I phoned Marjorie many, many times in the next few weeks. 'I can't stop you meeting now Fran, because I have given you her address, but we would advise you to wait,' she said.

'But it would finish me off if we didn't go ahead,' I pleaded, 'and the meeting would be a real pick-me-up.'

'OK Fran, if you're very determined, and your donor agrees, you can meet here on our premises as planned.'

Anne did agree, despite the impending procedure to harvest further white cells from her, and we both got ready for the big occasion. The lead up was incredible, my excitement and nervousness mounted, and I went through my entire wardrobe trying to decide what I could wear. I tried every outfit on for my poor nanny, and then Adrian took a day off and drove me to London. I was very worried in case we were late, but Adrian assured me we had plenty of time, and soon announced we were five minutes away.

Just then his mobile rang with a trivial call about his lawnmower, and while he talked he took a wrong turn and got lost in the heart of London, sending me into a blind panic. Eventually we found our way back, and I jumped out of the car to run into the office. Marjorie was waiting outside and announced 'Anne's here,' as she led me down the corridor. My heart was pounding with nervousness and I didn't know what on earth I was going to say. How could I find the right words to thank Anne for saving my life, and the chance she had given me of a future?

As Marjorie opened her door I saw Anne inside, and immediately noticed her caring smile. Then I saw she was crying, and she stepped towards me and we hugged. We both wept, and I don't even know what I said, or whether I spoke at all. After we let go of each other I looked her up and down, and she was everything I had dreamed of, a lovely, caring mum. She hugged Adrian and all the while Marjorie kept the conversation going. She was a tower of strength and announced she would take us to a pizza place where we could relax and get to know each other.

We sat at a table in the window and I began to learn things I had longed to know, like how it all began. Anne had worked for many years as a nurse on a children's ward and known many young patients with leukaemia and she had yearned to be a donor, but transplants were still in their infancy and Anne heard there weren't enough funds to handle the donor register. Anne continued to be bothered about the many children who couldn't find a match. Then, a few years before our transplant, she had watched a day-time TV show hosted by John Stapleton about people with leukaemia, and at the end an appeal had gone out for donors. Immediately she had picked up the phone and volunteered.

After she was confirmed as a donor match for me, Anne had been told there would be a delay before the transplant because I was pregnant. In the back of her mind she remembered me from a piece in the Anthony Nolan magazine and had a hunch she must be my donor. So all along she had guessed it was me.

We drank champagne and Anne described her bone marrow harvest and how her children messed around in the hospital room. The more she told me, the more I loved her.

We laughed a lot, especially on the return journey when Marjorie tore a huge rip across her long skirt on our car bumper. Back in the office she decided the only solution was to cut right across and convert the skirt from ankle-length to a mini. We took photos and it was a hilarious end to a perfect day. Anne was all that I had wanted her to be, like me, and with a genuine warmth.

Soon after our first meeting, the Hammersmith arranged for me to receive an injection of white blood cells from Anne. She was booked into the London clinic to give the blood which would be couriered to me in the Hammersmith. While we waited for the transfusion to arrive, Adrian and I had a coffee in the hospital café, and then walked back to the Dacie Ward to check whether the cells had arrived. We were amazed to bump into Anne in the corridor, who had come across London by tube after giving blood to wish me luck. I was bowled over by her kindness and struck by the weirdness of the situation – we hugged and then I walked on to receive her cells, already waiting on the ward.

The lymphocytes were given as an injection and I was able to go straight home. I hoped that at last my condition would come under control, and had no idea how much worse things were about to become.

During many of my visits to the Hammersmith that summer, I remembered the Duchess of Kent's promise that she would take me to Wimbledon one year after my transplant. I never expected it to come true, but out of the blue she sent me a little card inviting me to the tennis and mentioning that the three tenors happened to be performing at a Wembley concert after the ladies' finals, and would I like to join her for both events? Then I received the official invitation to sit in the Royal Box at Wimbledon. I simply could not believe this was happening to me.

I bought a brand new outfit and we set out on the Saturday of ladies' finals for the palace as instructed. The traffic was dreadful and when we arrived the official told us that the other guests were already waiting inside the royal apartment. He suggested we may like to bring our waterproof coats as the forecast for the evening concert was perfectly dreadful. Adrian and I had our old waxed jackets in the boot of the car, bought for our very first Christmas nine years earlier and worn to rags by dog walking.

'We can't possibly wear these!' I said, but the official suggested we really should have our waterproofs and that the Duchess would have hers too.

Then he showed us to the private quarters of the Palace, and we walked into the hallway clutching our dirty old coats. Katherine greeted us warmly and Adrian pointed out the Duke, who came to shake our hands. Then I noticed everybody else had curtsied, and I realised that I had let the side down by being clueless as usual. A minibus took us all to the tennis club where crowds of people were waiting to meet the Duchess, and I felt so odd stepping out of the bus onto the red carpet to meet the dignitaries on our way to a small private dining room for lunch.

When we were ushered into the Royal Box it was just as I have seen it a thousand times on the television, and Katherine had placed us on the very front row next to her. On my right I had the wife of the Wimbledon chairman and behind me the box was full of famous faces, Betty Boothroyd and people I recognised and realised I should have known. I couldn't concentrate on the tennis at all, but sat phased by the immensity of the occasion, and feeling the beautiful thick rug that was provided for each of us in case our knees felt chilly.

During afternoon tea I found myself sitting next to the Archbishop of Canterbury. It was another world, and I couldn't believe I was temporarily a part of it. We watched as Katherine went on to court to present the championship trophy, and then we changed our clothes before being taken to the open air concert. This time the minibus had a police escort to stop all the London traffic and allow us to pass, and Katherine apologised with embarrassment about the fuss. I peered out of the windows at passers-by and drivers who were trying to work out who was inside the bus, imagining their disappointment if they knew one of them was only me.

At Wembley I was introduced to John and Norma Major in the private function room, and then Katherine tapped me on the shoulder and asked me to meet Jeremy Irons and his wife Sinead Cusack. She had told them about my situation and they were extremely kind to me, genuinely interested in my story.

When the open-air concert began the heavens opened, just as the forecast predicted. Beside me, Katherine put on her waxed jacket, a beautiful new full-length one with a hood, and encouraged me to wear mine too. With utter embarrassment I wore my waist length stained coat, over the top of my new pink suit, and felt sure I wouldn't live it down. But the night was more special than I can describe, gradually the sky went dark and stars came out after the rain. The music seemed to come from another world, and I sat with tears streaming down my cheeks at the power and the glory of it all.

The Royal Minibus took us back to the Palace where Katherine hugged us goodnight on her doorstep. Adrian had booked a hotel room close to the Palace and we strolled to our beds, but were far too excited to sleep. After a late drink we sat up almost all night in our room, talking over every bit of the day we'll never forget.

I still found exertion very tiring and big events drained the little strength I had. During this same period Anthony Nolan invited me to attend their annual daisy ball, and then the leukaemia conference where I was asked to make a speech. The very thought terrified me, but Adrian coached and cajoled me and I finally agreed. It was the first of a series of public appearances, and that afternoon like all the occasions since, you could have heard a pin drop while I told my story. Without exception, then and since, people have reacted with great sympathy and interest, and I hope I have helped the medical profession to understand the illness from the other side of the fence.

We stayed a while to hear a couple of the medical speeches and I was fascinated to learn more about the equations that are done before a transplant takes place. I was already aware that for unknown reasons a transplant has a better chance of success with a young male donor. But the detail I heard that day would have made my heart go cold a year earlier, that if a donor is female it's preferable she has no children, is younger than 30 and that transplant happens less than a year after diagnosis. Anne was a mother, we were both over 30 and I had waited four years before my transplant. As I listened, I felt very lucky to be alive and realised statistics alone are meaningless.

That autumn Matthew started primary school, exactly a year after his first day at nursery, and Sebastian took his place. The day loomed large in my mind and I felt very emotional, so proud of them both, and recognising the huge achievement to have come so far as a Mum. But my heart broke as I knew I was losing my babies.

On Matthew's first day I managed to hold back my tears until he disappeared through the school door, then I broke down completely, crying for most of the day, with tears of sadness but also relief. All those long hours I imagined my boys at school, and replayed the miracle of their birth. If I had followed the advice of certain people, I would never have had Matthew or Sebastian and my story could have been utterly different. The realisation sank in, that I could be sitting at home a year after transplant with no children, and no hope of ever having any. That gap in my life would have been unfillable.

So many powerful thoughts went through my mind that autumn, which still haunt me now, the boys are my life and I want to be there for them every single minute, no one but me must get their PE kits together, or meet them after school. That's my role as their Mum, because I risked everything to have them, and I will always, always be there.

For all those times you stood by me,
for all the truth you made me see,
for all the joy you brought to my life,
for all the wrong that you made right,
for every dream you made come true,
for all the love I found in you.
I'll be for ever thankful, baby.

Lyrics from Céline Dion

Chapter Twenty

From Death to Life

CR ಶ CR ಶ

Despite my high hopes of a recovery after receiving white cells from Anne, throughout the following weeks my health seemed to deteriorate. During the autumn of 1996 I picked up every bug around, and was continually unwell with coughs and colds and found I was spending more and more time in bed

With the onset of winter I caught a bad cold and began to experience very severe pains in my chest that made it almost impossible to breathe. I continued to rest but the pain intensified with every breath.

By this time I had been fortunate enough to employ a cleaner, who helped with the housework I was no longer able to manage, and she has been an angel in my life. She was once a nun, and has become my friend and part of the family. One morning I came downstairs after resting and my cleaner was horrified to see my condition. She forced me to sit down, 'Something isn't right Fran, I'm sure this isn't normal. I think you may have pleurisy because if this was only 'flu you wouldn't have so much trouble breathing.'

The warning made me think I should take action, and when I phoned Dr White he asked to see me straight away, just as he's done throughout my illness. He checked me over, confirmed pleurisy and sent me home for complete rest.

But not long after I returned from the surgery he phoned me, 'Fran, I've been thinking about your case and I would like you to go to Heathcote Hospital and have an x-ray and a full check up. There's a chance you may have a blood clot and I want to eliminate that, I'm being extra cautious but in your case that's best.'

I drove to the hospital and x-rays were taken which I expected would close the subject. But back at home Dr White phoned again to say he had the result of the x-ray and had booked a bed for me in Warwick Hospital where I needed to have more tests to establish whether I had a pulmonary embolism on the lung. As soon as I reached the hospital I rang Mum and asked her to sit with me while I waited for the tests and then the results.

The wait seemed interminable and no doctor came to see me. The only bed space was on the geriatric ward and I was surrounded by frail old patients, most of them unconscious.

While I sat there I began to cry out of fear and despair that this may well be the end. I trawled through my mind for everything I had heard about a pulmonary embolism. I knew it is a blood clot that has become detached and travelled through the system to the lung. And I knew it is desperately serious, and that if I moved suddenly, or the clot travelled to the heart or brain, it would be instantly fatal. I had always thought if I was going to die it would be from leukaemia, I simply couldn't bear to be killed by a blood clot after all. By tea time I had become hysterical and Mum called Adrian to the hospital to comfort me.

As soon as he arrived he took charge of the situation. 'How long have you been waiting to see someone Fran?'

'All day, since first thing this morning.'

Adrian fetched a nurse, 'Fran needs to see a doctor immediately.'

Excuses were made but Adrian was adamant, 'If this is a pulmonary embolism, she has to be seen now.'

When a doctor finally came I told him I didn't want to stay on the geriatric ward where nothing could be done for me.

He said, 'You will stay here overnight and be transferred to the Walsgrave Hospital tomorrow for the scan to confirm a pulmonary embolism. The scan can only be done on a Friday or a Monday so if we don't get you in tomorrow you will have to wait here until next Monday.'

'I can't stay here, please,' I sobbed.

Adrian took charge again, 'I want to see someone higher up. We have private medical cover and if Fran has to stay in hospital all weekend, I want her transferred to the Chase where she can at least be comfortable.'

The nurses were very angry, but sent for the chest consultant, Dr Lawford Hill, who arrived at once and couldn't have been nicer. As soon as he heard about my leukaemia he said, 'Let's get you transferred to the Chase by ambulance right now, and I'll guarantee you an appointment at the Walsgrave first thing tomorrow. I fully understand why you're upset Fran. You're in a very precarious situation and we can't afford to take any chances with you.'

I felt a rush of gratitude and started to relax.

In hindsight I realise I was in total shock, and the ambulance transfer is just a hazy memory. I know Adrian went home to look after the boys and my parents sat with me that night.

In the morning I was taken by ambulance to the Walsgrave and was injected with a dye and scanned. Later that day Lawford Hill came to see me. 'Bad news, I'm afraid, you have got a pulmonary embolism. It's impossible to explain how it can have happened, maybe the white cell transfusion has caused a problem in your system, or perhaps it's the result of so much lying down recently. We'll never know why.'

I remained in hospital for several days and was given intravenous *Warfarin* in addition to the drugs I still had to take after transplant. I felt very, very depressed and truly feared for my life. Eventually I was sent home with a six month course of *Warfarin* and continued to visit the hospital for regular chest and blood checks. Dr Lawford Hill encouraged me to try and stay fit, and to keep my circulation going so I began a programme of exercise which I continue to this day. He told me you never know what is around the corner and that staying fit is the best advice anyone with my history could be given.

I made it through the winter and the spring and continued to have PCR chromosome tests which persisted in showing that I still had leukaemia.

Finally, on 18th April 1997, two years after my transplant, I had the phone call I had dreamed of for six long years. The Hammersmith rang with the result of my latest PCR test and told me they could no longer detect leukaemia. After the battle and the pain, it really was such simple news. The call came on my mother's birthday. In tears, I rang Adrian at once, then dashed into Warwick in a state of excitement. Instead of buying Mum a present as intended, I bought a little empty box and wrote inside on a scrap of paper in my spidery writing:

'This is an empty box to tell you that your birthday present is the news that the Hammersmith can no longer detect leukaemia.'

I wrapped it up, collected the boys from school and drove to Mum's. There were floods of tears that night and my brother Nick said on the phone, 'What a cop out, you didn't buy Mum a present!'

I phoned my mother-in-law, Joyce, who burst into tears on the phone. A few days later she was to send me a beautiful golden sovereign bracelet in the post with a note saying. 'This is for you because I am so astounded by your bravery throughout the last few years.'

We drank champagne for weeks and my blood count went to pieces, because I was banned from alcohol while taking *Warfarin,* but somehow it didn't seem to matter.

I still have PCR tests every three months and they continue to be negative, and that is as close to an all-clear as you get with leukaemia.

A few days later I was on a rare shopping trip with Dee in town and she grabbed my arm and practically dragged me into a record shop to listen to a song by Celine Dion. 'You've got to hear this,' she said, 'I know you'll want to buy it for Adrian, it's meant to be your song.'

We shared the headset and as soon as the lyrics began I started to weep. That set Dee off and we cried together in the record store, hearing the song that said the words I've never been able to string together for Adrian. That very night I gave the CD to him and the lyrics expressed what his love and support has meant to me.

> "You were my strength when I was weak,
> You were my voice when I couldn't speak,
>
> You were my eyes when I couldn't see,
> You saw the best there was in me,
>
> Lifted me up when I couldn't reach,
> You gave me faith cos you believed,
>
> I'm everything I am – because you loved me.
> You were always there for me,
>
> On tender wings you carried me,
> A light in the dark,
> Shining your love into my life"

And what of my donor? Anne and I have celebrated every anniversary of my transplant together, sometimes our two families spend the day at a theme park, or we stay for the weekend at one of our homes. One year we took all the children to a fair, and her son traded in his winning ticket for a present for me, a ring with a smiley face, the symbol that Anne and I still use as a code from the days when we couldn't sign our names. We call the transplant anniversary my birthday, and it's now a bigger celebration than my actual birthday, marking the date when Anne gave life back to me.

Eighteen months after my clear PCR test, my parents treated us to a holiday with them in Barbados, the place I had thought I'd never see again. I had less fear of travelling or picking up germs now, and knew the hotel was very clean.

In hindsight, the holiday was unique, an oasis before the storm that was to break with my brother's diagnosis only two months later. For the first time in years our family had no worries, and there were no clouds over our horizon.

During the holiday we celebrated Sebastian's fifth birthday, and while he opened his presents on the soft sandy beach, suddenly around the corner wandered a lovely native man whom Adrian and I met years before and always hoped to find again. He made souvenirs out of palm leaves for tourists, and he popped up on Sebastian's special day. We asked him to make a birthday hat, and all watched in amazement as he measured Sebastian's head and fashioned a perfect boater from thick green leaves. Sebastian was more delighted than he had ever been with an expensive toy and still has the hat.

That night we took the boys for a meal at a restaurant on the beach, and we chose an open-air table on the decking. Because it was a special occasion, we allowed the boys to play with Grandma and Grandpa on the sand while our meals were prepared.

The sun was just setting in a wide sweep of peach and gold, across the expanse where sky met sea, and I cupped my wine glass in my hand as I looked at the unforgettable scene.

Below me, at the edge where the waves lapped the sand, my beautiful, precious sons played together, Sebastian's new hat silhouetted by the golden sea. I could hear the boys' babbling chatter as they dipped into the water, and I gazed at my dear parents watching over them. Dad sat very close to

Mum on the sand, and they were looking at their grandsons with complete love, pride and peace.

'A penny for them,' Adrian said to me.

But I couldn't speak, and tears just welled up and brimmed over onto my cheeks. It was all too much joy, I felt more happiness than I could bear.

'I know,' he said gently, smiling at me with a face reflecting the golden glow of the setting sun, 'we're very, very lucky.'

It was weird, but deep down inside me, buried below the joy, something about the scene tugged at my heart-strings with an inexpressible sadness. I couldn't get to the bottom of it, perhaps it was an echo to the bittersweet of the night in Antigua when Matthew was conceived, and whatever the cause, it troubled my soul.

* * *

Ever since diagnosis my fascination had remained with the old film *Love Story* that had been my only prior knowledge of leukaemia. But I had never dared to get out the video.

Very recently I found myself alone at home and decided to watch the film for the first time in twenty-five years. As soon as the title music began to play, I started to weep, uncontrollably and without end. I had forgotten the opening scene, but it came back to me now with a force that I felt physically. Ryan O'Neal sat on a bench and his voice-over spoke, 'What can you say about a twenty-five year old girl who loved Mozart, Bach and the Beatles, and who has died?'

With a bolt to the core, I understood. This was it, the source of pain that has tugged so hard at every moment of great happiness in the past twelve years: the strain of more than a decade of treatment, and the loss of my brother broke over me.

Something began to make sense at last as I watched *Love Story*, and let all my grief and fear pour out. The words sank in – what indeed can you say about losing someone you love? I had lost my first child, and my brother, and had stood at the jaws of death myself. I had watched my husband, mother and father suffer agonies of grief and terror, but had never allowed myself to feel the rawness of it. For me the entire illness had been played out behind a protective barrier of numbness.

And now I was imposing a barrier on getting well, never daring to believe I was free of leukaemia, feeling too worthless and too afraid to let my recovery be real. From the moment of diagnosis I had been dying to live, but since transplant I had been too frightened to seize my chance of life.

But as I sat, washed empty and bare by the tears *Love Story* had unleashed, I knew I'd made a new beginning. I could still hold on to my faith in the power of love and healing.

Out of my emptiness, just as real and absolute as I had felt in the Dacie Ward six years earlier, a new emotion was born. For the sake of Nick and all those who have stood by me in love, I was ready to allow myself to live.

Only YOU could save a life...

Thousands of people die every year from fatal bone marrow diseases. Like Fran, they desperately need a blood stem cell transplant from an unrelated donor in order to survive. These people are relying on strangers to save their lives.

YOU COULD BE THAT MATCH

You may be the only person in the world who could match.

If you are in good health, weigh over 8 stone and are aged between 18-40, The Anthony Nolan Trust needs you NOW. Males and ethnic minorities are needed even more desperately. Joining The Anthony Nolan Trust register will cost nothing, but not acting quickly and sharing what is unique to you could cost a life.

Please contact The Trust on:

Telephone: **020 7284 1234**
E-mail: **(individuals)**
newdonor@anthonynolan.com
(corporate/group recruitment)
kayc@anthonynolan.com
Website: **www.anthonynolan.org.uk**
Address: **The Anthony Nolan Trust,**
PO BOX 1767,
London NW3 4YR

THANK YOU